1 Willy Lott's Cottage, Flatford Mill, Suffolk: detail of
John Constable's *The Hay-Wain*

THE NATIONAL TRUST

A Record of Fifty Years' Achievement

WITH AN INTRODUCTION BY
G. M. TREVELYAN, O.M.

AND CONTRIBUTIONS BY

IVOR BROWN	JAMES LEES-MILNE
HARRY BATSFORD	BASIL OLIVER
GRAHAME CLARK	JOHN SUMMERSON
JOHN H. HARVEY	JOHN RUSSELL
G. M. YOUNG	D. M. MATHESON

SIR WILLIAM BEACH THOMAS

EDITED BY
JAMES LEES-MILNE

B. T. BATSFORD LTD.
15 NORTH AUDLEY STREET, LONDON, W.1

To the Memory of
MISS OCTAVIA HILL
CANON RAWNSLEY
and
SIR ROBERT HUNTER
Founders of The National Trust

First Published Summer, 1945

MADE AND PRINTED IN GREAT BRITAIN
BY JARROLD AND SONS LIMITED, NORWICH

CONTENTS

PREFACE

THIS book is meant to give a bare outline of what the National Trust has achieved throughout the fifty years of its existence, and of the varied types of properties it holds.

It has been found impracticable to distinguish every single Trust-owned property mentioned in the text from other properties mentioned, but not so owned. In the first place the very great majority of the place names occurring in the following chapters do actually belong to the Trust. To offset any confusion, however, a careful index has been provided at the end of the book, identifying in distinct types those properties owned and those protected by covenants. In case of difficulty, readers are asked to refer to this index. Not every National Trust property, of course, has been included in this book, which has sought to avoid a mere catalogue of place names. Those requiring a complete list are strongly advised to become members—if they are not already—for they will be supplied with the National Trust's Handbook of Properties, annually brought up to date.

It is not perhaps inopportune to specify here a few of the privileges of Trust membership. First and foremost members have the satisfaction of helping to preserve the traditional face of their country, and some at least of its national monuments. Free admission is granted to all Trust properties where a charge is otherwise made to non-members. Members are furthermore eligible for special dinners, luncheons and receptions and visits organized in normal times to places not generally open to the public. A quarterly journal, the Annual Report and the illustrated Handbook of Properties are issued to them. Lastly, members have the right to a vote in the affairs of the Trust.

What, on the other hand, are some of the privileges of the Trust itself? The Trust enjoys statutory powers to hold land and buildings inalienably and for all time. Property given or left by will to the Trust and held for preservation is excluded from death duties and aggregation with the rest of the benefactor's estate. The Trust has special powers to protect privately owned land and buildings by means of restrictive covenants, and special powers to collaborate with local authorities with a view to preservation generally. The Trust has its own bye-laws to control and regulate its properties. These are but a few of its privileges.

The constitutional fabric of the Trust has not varied since its inauguration in the distant nineties. The President and Chairman of the Council is to-day H.M. Queen Mary, actually the fourth holder of this office. The Council, which is composed of fifty members (one half nominated by different learned bodies, the other elected by the members of the Trust at each Annual Meeting), appoints its Executive Committee. The Chairman of the Executive Committee is the Marquess of Zetland, K.G. The Executive Committee in its turn appoints a number of Sub-Committees. Chief of these are the Finance and General Purposes Committee, whose Chairman is Viscount Esher, and the Estates Management Committee, whose Chairman is Dr. G. M. Trevelyan, O.M.

It is particularly appropriate that Dr. Trevelyan has written his inspiring introduction to this brief chronicle of the National Trust's fifty years. For, as well as being the most distinguished of our living historians, Dr. Trevelyan is a benefactor of the Trust of long standing, and consequently no one is better qualified to estimate its past achievements and its future title in the post-war world. The other contributors have found time from their several exacting war duties to pay splendid tribute to that aspect of the Trust's work, of which each is an expert assessor.

Finally, I dare to extend a word of gratitude to that quarter where it is least expected yet most deserved, namely to Mr. Charles Fry of Batsford, for supplementing those virtues essential in the production of a book of this kind—patience, efficiency and humour.

J. L-M.

June, 1945.

ACKNOWLEDGEMENT

THE Publishers are indebted to the Trustees of the National Gallery for permission to reproduce the detail of Constable's *Hay Wain*, used as the frontispiece; to the National Museum of Wales, for Fig. 37; to Messrs. Jonathan Cape, Ltd., for Fig. 31, from *Bodiam Castle*, by the late Lord Curzon; and to the Marquess of Northampton, for kindly supplying the print of the picture in his collection reproduced on Fig. 100.

As regards the photographs, they are indebted to G. P. Abraham, for Fig. 9; the Ashmolean Museum, for Figs. 25 and 27 (from the collection of the late Major G. W. G. Allen); Associated Press, for Fig. 103; W. J. B. Blake, for Figs. 6, 11, 12, 15; the British Council, for Figs. 4, 17, 19, 21, 34, 44, 78, 79, 80, 81, 86, 88, 94, 112 (from the collection of J. Dixon-Scott); the late Brian C. Clayton, for Figs. 29, 30, 35, 41, 91; Country Life, Ltd., for Figs. 3, 42, 49, 55, 62, 63, 64, 65, 70, 71, 72, 73, 74, 75, 76, 77, 92, 95; Herbert Felton, for Figs. 85, 87, 90, 93; F. Frith & Co., for Fig. 7; Leonard and Marjorie Gayton, for Figs. 2, 5, 24, 40, 45, 82, 104; Messrs. Gibson & Sons, Penzance, for Fig. 89; T. Russell Goddard, for Figs. 106, 108, 110; D. J. Hallaghan, for Fig. 46; J. Hardman, for Fig. 10; Humphrey and Vera Joel, for Figs. 56, 57, 58, 59; A. F. Kersting, for Fig. 98; Lesley Lawrence, for Fig. 67; Dorien Leigh, Ltd., for Figs. 16 and 54; N. Lloyd, for Figs. 68 and 69; the Mustograph Agency, for Figs. 22 and 36; the Duchess of Northumberland, for Figs. 107 and 109; Messrs. Pearson & Sons, Shaftesbury, for Fig. 14; the Photocrom Co., for Fig. 8; *Picture Post*, for Fig. 102; Niall Rankin, for Fig. 105; R. G. Spiller, Taunton, for Figs. 57, 58, 59; John Stacey, for Fig. 111; Will F. Taylor, for Figs. 23, 47, 51, 60, 101; *The Times*, for Figs. 13, 18, 48; F. R. Winstone, for Figs. 28, 32, 33; and Major Richard Wyndham, for Fig. 20. The remaining subjects are taken from the collections of the National Trust and of the Publishers.

Finally, they must record their grateful thanks to Sir John Dashwood, Bt., for permitting them, at great personal inconvenience, to reproduce the picture in his collection which forms the jacket.

INTRODUCTION

By G. M. Trevelyan, o.m.

Chairman of the Estates Committee of the National Trust

It is the Jubilee Year of the National Trust, founded fifty years ago by Miss Octavia Hill, Sir Robert Hunter and Canon Rawnsley. This volume contains a series of brief essays by a number of distinguished and able writers, all of them cognizant of the work of the Trust in one or another of its aspects. They endeavour to place that work in proper perspective, by relating it to the national inheritance as a whole, and to the general situation as regards preservation of natural beauty and historic buildings.

In the present age there is, I think, a more widespread appreciation of natural beauty and of historic buildings than ever before, and much more conscious desire on the part of city dwellers to take their holidays in unspoiled country. Holidays with pay and the Youth Hostels Association with its membership of 130,000 climbers, walkers and cyclists are cheering signs of the times. On the other hand never before was the destruction of natural beauty going on at such a pace by uncontrolled development; and the break-up of country houses and the grounds surrounding them is one of the social facts of the age. The country houses and their grounds, as private possessions, are in very many cases doomed by the system of taxation. And natural scenery in its wider aspects is attacked by the builder and by government departments and municipal authorities in their search for land for utilitarian purposes. In time of war the builder of bungalows is under restraint, but government departments are even more active in their depredations than in time of peace.

Some of this is inevitable. The island is too small. But the scramble for the precious land ought to be controlled by some authority that would give consideration to amenity as one of the objects to be held in view when possible. Unfortunately this does not occur, and in the ordinary course, each department of government takes what it likes without remorse or consultation. Only occasionally public protest saves a situation at the last moment. There ought to be a more efficacious system for co-ordinating the claims of the various utilitarian interests and relating them to the preservation of natural beauty and of the holiday grounds of the people.

This is not done. There is indeed talk about planning the whole island, and talk about National Parks, but it is only talk about a possible future, and meanwhile destruction goes on apace, whether in war or in peace.

In these unhappy circumstances, the National Trust plays a considerable part in the much restricted movement, carried on by private initiative, for the preservation of the national heritage of beauty. Yet the sphere of the Trust's action is still pitifully small—only 110,000 acres owned by the Trust and some 40,000 more protected by covenants with the Trust in the whole of England, Wales and Northern Ireland. But it is a great deal better than nothing, for the acreage so protected contains much fine scenery and many places and buildings of great beauty and interest.

The National Trust is not the only worker in the cause of preservation. Besides local bodies such as the Friends of the Lake District and the Norfolk Naturalists' Trust there are four great national societies, the Commons and Footpaths Preservation Society, the Society for the Protection of Ancient Buildings, the Council for the Preservation of Rural England, and the Scapa Society for restraint of disfiguring advertisements. With all these, the National Trust fully co-operates. The C.P.R.E. carries on specifically the work of propaganda and of protests, sometimes successful, against particular acts of intended vandalism. The special function of the National Trust is different. It is the ownership and care of the properties committed to its charge. Its geographical area is England, Wales and Northern Ireland. There is a similar but quite separate Scottish National Trust which is doing, with great success, similar work in North Britain.

There is indeed one way in which the State helps to preserve our historic heritage. The Ancient Monuments section of the Ministry of Works does excellently in maintaining many ruins of castles, abbeys, etc. But that depart-ment is not allowed to save houses still inhabited and unruined, and therefore cannot help with the solution of what we may call the country house problem. The relation of the National Trust with the Ancient Monuments section of the Ministry of Works is most friendly, and mutual help is exchanged.

Properties come to the National Trust in various ways, often by gift or by bequest, and often by purchase, financed either by some single benefactor or by public subscription.

The Trust has to make it a rule not to accept a property unless it is self-supporting. Some properties can pay for their own maintenance, not a few by agricultural rents or by the letting value of a house, or by gate money raised from the visiting public, as at Housesteads (Borcovicus), its fort upon the Roman Wall. But if a property has no such intrinsic annual value, the Trust must ask for an endowment in money for its maintenance. This rule is absolutely necessary for financial solvency, but its application often causes disappointment both to the would-be donor and to the Trust.

Recent legislation has enabled much to be done through covenants. An owner who wishes to keep the rent and proprietorship of an area of land, but is ready to part with its development value either by gift or by sale, can enter into a covenant with the Trust whereby the Trust will for all time to come have the right of veto or control of building or any other possible developments on the land in question. In this way as many as 40,000 acres are already protected, including such fine areas as Buttermere Valley.

In the management of its properties the Trust endeavours to avoid the evils of bureaucracy and over-centralization. It has a flexible system, not uniform in all the various properties scattered over the country. Some are managed by local committees, of course in close touch with the Trust's agents. But some local committees are advisory only. And for yet another class of property, usually a small one, there is no local committee and the management rests entirely with the officers of the Trust. In order to prevent centralizing things too much on the London office, it is establishing a system of Regional Agents,

2 Lacock Village, Wiltshire

3 St. John's Jerusalem, Sutton-at-Hone, Kent

4 Princes Risborough Manor House, Buckinghamshire

whole-time servants of the Trust and imbued with its ideals, resident each in his allotted Region, but working under the Head Agent, Mr. Hubert Smith. This system cannot cover the whole country until demobilization releases the men we need. But it is even now largely operative. Indeed for a number of years before the war the most important group of properties, those in the Lake District, were already under the control of the Regional Agent up there, Mr. Bruce Thompson, aided on some properties by strong local committees. As in this case, a Regional Agent of the Trust must always be, not merely a business land agent, but also a man endowed with the love of natural beauty and sym-pathetic with the local spirit and with the point of view of the farmers and other tenants and friends of the Trust in his Region.

The Trust also wishes to avoid turning its properties into "beauty spots" or "museum pieces". Its object is that natural beauty should remain "natural" and that agriculture should continue to flourish as agriculture.

Undoubtedly many very difficult problems of litter, camping, hostels and other accommodation will arise increasingly as a consequence of the spill-over into the country of more and yet more holiday-makers from the town. Box Hill after a fine week-end yields the scriptural "twelve baskets full" of "fragments that remain". Sometimes gates are left open and sometimes hayfields are walked through regardless of farming interests. Yet I am not without hope of the gradual education of the mass of visitors as their holidays in the country become more frequent. The experience of the Youth Hostels Association and other such bodies is that those whom they bring into the countryside, particu-larly walkers, are learning to respect nature and also to respect and understand the farmer and his work. I have some hope that this war and its sequel will teach the townee that food is not an import obtainable in shops as a matter of course, but a thing produced by skill and labour in the countryside and that the countryside is not only the holiday ground for the visitor from the town, but is also the workshop of the farmer.

But the need to preserve natural beauty, both by the National Trust and other-wise, is not merely a question of preserving holiday grounds for masses of people from the town. It is also a matter of preserving a main source of spiritual wellbeing and inspiration, on which our ancestors throve and which we are in danger of losing for ever. The two objects indeed are hardly to be distinguished. For the value of the holiday ground as such depends not merely on supplying air and exercise to the city worker, but on offering him the spiritual delight and sustenance that he cannot get in the modern city, so completely divorced from nature. We are literally "children of the earth", and removed from her our spirit withers or runs to various forms of insanity. Unless we can refresh ourselves at least by intermittent contact with nature, we grow awry.

This flag of beauty, hung out by the mysterious universe, to claim the worship of the heart of man, what is it, and what does its signal mean to us? There is no clear interpretation. But that does not lessen its value. Like the universe, like life, natural beauty also is a mystery. But whatever it may be, whether casual in its origin as some hold who love it well, or whether, as others hold, such splendour can be nothing less than the purposeful message of God—

whatever its interpretation may be, natural beauty is the ultimate spiritual appeal of the universe, of nature, or of the God of nature, to their nursling man.   It and it alone makes a common appeal to the sectaries of all our religious and scientific creeds, to the lovers of all our different schools of poetry and art, ancient and modern, and to many more beside these.   It is the highest common denominator in the spiritual life of to-day.

Yet now that it is most consciously valued, it is being most rapidly destroyed upon this planet, and above all in this island.   In old days it needed no con-servation.   Man was camped in the midst of it and could not get outside it, still less destroy it.   Indeed, until the end of the eighteenth century the works of man only added to the beauty of nature.   But science and machinery have now armed him with weapons that will be his own making or undoing, as he chooses to use them;   at present he is destroying natural beauty apace in the ordinary course of business and economy.   Therefore, unless he now will be at pains to make rules for the preservation of natural beauty, unless he consciously protects it at the partial expense of some of his other greedy activities, he will cut off his own spiritual supplies, and leave his descendants a helpless prey forever to the base materialism of mean and vulgar sights.

This matter has become a public question of the first magnitude.   The value of natural beauty is admitted in words by our public men, but when it comes to deeds the doctrine is too new to bear much fruit.   It has for centuries been held sacrilege to destroy a church.   But a place of natural beauty may be destroyed, and is often so taxed by the State that it must be sold to the jerry-builder. Meanwhile, the State itself pours forth the money of ratepayer and taxpayer for the perpetration all over the island of outrages on the beauty of the country. Those who mourn over the destruction of abbeys long ago, should look also at the beam in our own eye, and hasten to save from destruction or disfigurement parks, woodlands and valley heads.

This is a civic duty that cannot any longer be neglected without dire con-sequences. Destruction walks by noonday. Unless the State reverses the engines and instead of speeding up destruction, plans the development of the country so that the minimum of harm can be done to beauty, the future of our race, whatever its social, economic and political structure may be, will be brutish and shorn of spiritual value.

To this great work of salvage, the National Trust makes at least a contribution.

I

NATIONAL TRUST AND NATIONAL PARKS

By Ivor Brown

ONE sentence, whose author, I must confess, I cannot remember, has summed up the qualities and duties of two epochs with a brevity and acumen beyond criticism. "It was the function of the nineteenth century to liberate: it will be the function of the twentieth to control."

Control is now a word under suspicion. To the individualists it has an evil smell. But it is hardly denied by anyone that the Age of Anyhow, as Lord Baldwin has so simply and so well defined the nineteenth century, demands for successor an Age of Order. In the Anyhow period the gates of productivity were open and the expanding markets of the world eagerly awaited the emerging flood; wealth and numbers multiplied, though not always in the same streets; development exploited, enriched and often defiled the land. The British rich had discovered and rented Scotland and the London (later New York) laird was monarch of the glen. The British poor were not expected, at least in Dickens's time, to take holidays. They were of the town and could stay there. They might, perhaps, take the steamer to Margate or walk as far as the local gin-palace. But Dingley Dell expected no streams of "hikers" to disturb its autumn partridges or come tramping through its Christmas revels. The country in Dickens, never so actual as the town, was invaded only by the Dedlocks. The Wilfers were not greatly interested in the wind on the heath: in any case, if they wanted country views they had only to look out of a Somers Town window towards the bosky knolls of Highgate or survey the undulant meadows of Hampstead from one of those north-westerly gardens still existing in front of the houses in the Euston Road, in which position they were set to act as belvederes. These strips are scarcely gardens now, but they were pleas-ances in those far-off, pre-railway days: here London stopped and a Londoner sat on his lawn with an unbroken view of the northern heaths and woodlands.

But the problem of holidays and countryside and access had soon to be faced. Even Hampstead Heath itself had to be saved from enclosure. Else-where the nabobs of the new finance were following the example of the old nobility by fencing in this and closing up that. As early as 1865 it was found necessary to begin the Preservation Process. First, in 1865, came the Society to protect Commons, Open Spaces, and Footpaths. Birds were next on the protected list (1889). In 1895 came the National Trust, then a mere David against that huge Goliath of urban "spilth" which threatened to overwhelm the places of natural beauty and historic interest richly clustering our island. The National Trust's function was at once simple and double: to keep despoilers out and to let enjoyers in. It sought to shut the gates on the unruly vandal and to open them for the decent citizen.

No better, no more natural start could have been made than in the Lake District, where Canon Rawnsley, one of the three main founders of the Trust, had set his heart as well as his home. This area has the highest English mountains as well as the fairest English dales: it is nobly ghosted, from Southey's Keswick to Wordsworth's Grasmere and Hawkshead and Ruskin's Coniston. With its superb mixture of crag and canyon, of forest, mere and scree it was the proper frame for the Romantic Movement in its English phase. And because the Lakes were so remote, so truly rural, and so calming to the soul they evoked especially the English spirit. This, after a brief French flirtation, soon divorced that general surging of the human mind from alien, and violent uprising and matched the new romance of revolution with the old prudence, preferring the tolerant (and even Tory) ways of thought. The Lakes were, as John Burns said of the Thames, liquid history: they were a geographical unit. They became the natural target of the new, huge holiday-making crowds, who, no longer abhorring the savagery of nature as was the eighteenth-century fashion and now enfranchised with cheap transport and the recently invented "week-end", were flowing out of the Coketowns to find, to enjoy, and possibly to overrun the much appreciated beauty-spot. (Beauty-spot in the Oxford English Dictionary is defined as a spot or patch placed upon the face by ladies: later it was to be a spot or patch placed upon the face of an agreeable landscape and selected for profitable cultivation by owners of garages, tea-rooms and kiosks.) Furthermore the rapid railway services arranged between Windermere and Manchester were turning Winander's green and pleasant banks into a convenient dormitory for the wealthier owners of Lancashire's dark satanic mills.

The first achievements of that National Trust were modest enough. To me, on my first youthful visit to the Lakes, made in the autumn of 1911, the Trust was a stranger and the discovery of a notice-board marking some small Trust lands in Borrowdale came as a happy surprise. But the process of acquisition sped and spread. Notable advances included that particular prize, the Scafell area with all the finest Cumbrian peaks. These were made public forever, surely a shining example of Wordsworth's "joy in widest commonalty spread", as memorials to men fallen in the 1914-18 war. By purchase and by donation the Trust properties, or land over which it held a restrictive covenant, grew splendidly. By 1939 the Trust actually owned 11,000 acres in this region and had 14,000 more protected from "development". Within the following six years the figures have risen to 18,000 acres owned and 17,000 protected.

Now this progress of public possession and protection within one especially beautiful area, an area moreover marked off by natural formation as a distinct unit of North-Western England, coincided with the dispersion of another but similar idea, that of the National Park. If England was to enjoy one or more of these National Parks, the Lake District seemed an obvious choice for a beginning. For here so many crannies and expanses of desirable land and water were already, in one sense, national.

National Parks, internationally regarded, were a great deal older than our National Trust itself. Other nations had realized that the Age (and methods)

5   The Vale of Newlands, near Keswick, in the Lake District

6   The Manifold Valley, Staffordshire

of Anyhow might be fatal to landscape, to wild life, and to the survival of territory in anything like its natural condition. The U.S.A. had started its great Yellowstone Park in 1872, and similar great reserves, some of them specifically game preserves, were begun by Canada in addition to the U.S.A., by South Africa, Australia, and the Belgian Congo as well as by many countries in Europe. There may seem to be no obvious parallel between a reservation made for the safety of the greater mammals, with shooting permitted only under strict surveillance, and the control of British fell-sides for the benefit of urban ramblers. But the principle of public control with public access is the same and essential, even though it is not everybody who will passionately assert his right of entry to a jungle otherwise maintained for the freedom and felicity of lions. Great Britain might seem, from the smallness of its area and the largeness of its towns, to be in particular need of National Parks. But so far it has only made a small beginning with National Forest Parks, that is to say by encouraging access to the unplanted fringe of the big afforestations laid out by the Forestry Commissioners.

It is obvious from the above that there is no exact definition, as yet, of a National Park. But we are confronted here with something far more definite than a merely pleasant idea. The following, very useful specification was made in a pamphlet called "The Case for National Parks in Great Britain", issued by the Standing Committee on National Parks in 1938. (This Committee was formed to represent all the bodies interested in the public enjoyment and preservation of Britain's natural resources.)

"A National Park may be defined, in broad terms, as an extensive district of beautiful wilder landscape, strictly preserved in its natural aspect and kept or made widely accessible for public enjoyment and open-air recreation, including particularly cross-country walking, while continued in its traditional farming use. Thus a National Park is not the same thing as a local or regional 'green belt' or 'open space'—not merely because it must ordinarily be more extensive and more specifically concerned with wilder landscape but also because it must be of significance and service to the nation as a whole. By comparison, green belts and open spaces may be largely made up of ordinary farm land and are essentially the concern of the large towns to which they are related. Still more is a National Park quite different from a town park, although they have a common and somewhat misleading name."

Furthermore it is emphasized that a National Park is not a nature reserve, but may very well contain one. Nor is it, necessarily, a piece of nationalized or "National-Trusted" land. It would probably ease administration very greatly if all the land for which a future National Parks Commission becomes responsible were owned publicly. But the condition is not essential. In many of the places most desirable as National Parks there are landowners who are proud of their property, often long held by their family: they have administered it well, no doubt, and they may feel that they have mixed their love and labour so closely with their soil and houses that parting would be more than sorrow. These owners would understandingly resent compulsory public purchase, even if that were enacted for the best and most social purposes. So long as they do not sell to undesirable successors or restrict access to the hills, why should a National Parks Commission interfere with them? All that is wanted is control, for the simple and double purpose aforesaid, to keep the despoilers out and let the enjoyers in. If the owners are sympathetic to the double purpose and if they are pledged to regard the conditions proper to a National Park, they should be allowed to remain. At least, that is one point of view.

For this is the important fact to remember. No great upheaval, disturbance, or railing off is contemplated. A National Park would be natural country. The title is rather unfortunate in its suggestion of trimmed lawns, bandstands, railings, bye-laws and tea-pavilions on a grandiose scale. That, indeed, is the very last thing that National-Parkers have in mind. What they want is that bits of Britain should remain bits of Britain, with their birds, animals, trees and flowers unmolested, their indigenous agriculture and their crafts continuing, their herds on the hills and their hay-fields in the dales.

The "beauty-spot" conception is fundamentally odious to a good National-Parker. For this conception selects a single feature or nook in a whole and handsome landscape, preferably that feature or nook which contains the most conventional ingredients of picture-postcard picturesqueness, item one mountain with peak, item one lake with waterfall, item one islet with trees, and then concentrates all the attention of the visitors on this corner. To this extent the beauty-spot may be a blessing. It masses together in one agglomeration of hotels, cafés, petrol-pumps, memento-shops, boat-houses, booths and what you will, all those who like beauty-spots but are completely bored by beauty. These latter have neither the will nor the vigour to wander far afield and so the more active people, who have a larger vision and affection for country, can rely upon finding comparative solitude at no more than half a mile from the little hive of "tourisme" where the beauty-spotting drones are blissfully swarming. I have previously (and a little playfully, but not, I think, altogether foolishly) advocated a State supply of scheduled beauty-spots for the benefit of those who really enjoy beauty. These latter, list in hand, would know exactly what to avoid and the "out-for-a-nice-spin" motorist and "office-outing" motor-coach loads would know exactly what to seek. The best of good times, assorted, would be had by all.

But we are wandering out of our National Park. This, it was insisted, would be natural country with its ordinary work unimpeded, and, if possible, assisted, by the National Parks Commission. This would presumably be set up by Act of Parliament to administer specified National Parks areas in association with the existing local and planning authorities, but possessing a wider territorial scope and some necessarily stronger powers in order to prevent various forms of restriction and aggression. The main restriction to be feared and fought is refusal of access to mountains because of possible damage to shooting-rights by disturbance of game. The possible aggressions are many. Mining and quarrying without carefully planned schemes to limit and remedy surface devastation, commercial afforestation with monotonous soft-wood plantations, water-catchment schemes, flooding of valleys to make reservoirs, dam-building, overhead cables, and hydro-electric developments involving huge exposed pipe-lines, new power-stations and shabby housing for the workers are all dangers to which the best of our mountain country has recently been exposed.

National Park enthusiasts, we must repeat, are not trying to sterilize the country or make a museum of a mountain-range by opposing all such plans for using the nation's "white coal", that is, its water-power, or the rock from which the wild beauty of the surface and the sky-line has been wrought by the contortions of the æons. They insist, however, that all such schemes must be carefully watched and, if necessary, checked in order to prevent gross wastage of the limited solitude and splendour that our small islands contain. Little local authorities may easily be won over by promises of "prosperity" and bigger rateable values. They may be careless, possibly even corrupt. In any case, their powers and their areas may be too small to cope with any big approach by "big business" or by one of the new semi-public corporations engaged on "development". Then there are always the fighting services, in search of training grounds, aerodromes, bomb-practice targets and so on. It is note-worthy that in the Annual Report of the Friends of the Lake District, issued in 1944, the recorded conflicts of this excellent group of protectors were far more with public bodies and departments than with the private vandal. A National Parks Commission, it cannot be too strongly insisted, would be in a much better position to fight the necessary defensive actions than would a number of small and possibly jealous local authorities. "It was the function of the nineteenth century to liberate: it will be the function of the twentieth to control." The National Parks Commission would be constantly visualizing the double purpose, to liberate and control the countryside for its best usage as a source of wealth as well as of recreation.

The National Park, as I conceive it, is a proper extension of the idea of the National Trust. It will preserve, for the general public, the place of natural beauty and historic interest, but it will at all times seek to maintain the rights of the local public to use their own place for its own wealth-yielding purposes in familiar and traditional ways. It would be easiest to begin with a nucleus of National Trust property, some famous hills, woods, or waters and then, by means of the Park, to put a kind of cordon round this central excellence, working according to the lie of the land and using the units which geography has created. The Lake District must plainly be one Park, if Parks we can have. There is already a belt of country, including the grandest peaks, stretch-ing in a south-easterly direction right across this glorious area, from Loweswater to Windermere, by way of Buttermere, to the Scafells, Bow Fell, and the Langdales, which is firmly and almost continuously held by the Trust, either as owned or covenant-protected land. Together with big holdings on Ulls-water and by Ambleside and many scattered units this makes a superb nucleus for a surrounding Lake District Park.

Derbyshire offers similar opportunities, both in the Buxton area and in the valleys of the Dove and Manifold. In both these regions the Trust is well established and the nucleus ready. Moreover in this case the menace to fine wild country in the north and to the exquisite "clouds" (as the hills are often called) and clefts in the limestone to the south is a serious one. For a glance at the map will show that Dovedale and the Manifold are closely encircled by immense and crowded industrial areas, the Potteries, Derby and Nottingham, Chesterfield, Sheffield, Rotherham and Barnsley, with the vast sprawl of Manchester and its suburbs away on the north-west. The moors round Buxton are, I believe, within sixty miles of half the population of England, being swiftly approached from the huge "conurbations" of South and Central Yorkshire and South and Central Lancashire as well as from the North Midland industrial belt already mentioned. This is not only an obvious danger to rural Derbyshire: it is a chance to serve the vital needs of this huge population in the promised age of popular leisure and of holidays for all. But, if protection and service are to go together, plainly vigilance will be essential and a Peak Park with Dovedale and the Manifold included or two separate Derbyshire Parks will be required. The strip of mountain between the Sheffield and Manchester urban groupings is narrow and in places tightly held against ramblers. Access here is an acute problem and strong measures, i.e., National Park legislation, may be required in order to get it. The need is plain and paramount.

From Derbyshire to the north the enthusiasts for a Pennine Way hope to develop a public track which will go right up this central and superb roof-top of England from Edale to the Cheviots, thus enabling the knapsack traveller to take the high road to Scotland in quite a new manner. Whether it would be necessary to "empark" this territory is uncertain. The nucleus, admittedly, is not there, Trust holdings being few between Ripon and the Roman Wall. But a scheme for a West Riding Regional Park, has been prepared by Col. W. S. Cameron of Leeds and it might be prudent, before mechanized civilization marches on, to regard as likely areas for protection the magnificent reaches of Upper Teesdale, including the great waterfalls of High Force and Cauldron Snout with the huge expanse between Middleton, Appleby and Alston, and the region of the Roman Wall itself.

In North Wales the Snowdon group suggests itself at once. It is a distinct unit. It is unique in height and grandeur among the mountains south of the Scottish border. It is easily available from South Lancashire and the Midlands and much less easily from South Wales, but Wales will not endure its vile communications between north and south. There, it is true, Trust holdings are few. Fortunately access is fairly general. Poor "sport" makes good walking. Snowdon is lucky to have no grouse or deer. As to desirable parks in Central and South Wales, opinions will differ. If we are to include coastal areas of special wildness and beauty as ripe for this kind of protection, then the noble cliffs and bays of Pembrokeshire must be the first beneficiary. The Trust has here its excellent points of vantage. Inland there is a large mountainous expanse between the Wye and the Towy offering glorious holidays to the men of the southern valleys and therefore asking at the same time for the kind of protection that the status of a National Park could bestow.

Crossing the Bristol Channel we find Exmoor a National Park unit equipped with a fine cluster of Trust properties from Bideford running east over Dunkery to Bridgwater. Dartmoor to the south is another natural unit of grand country with especial prehistoric interest, but as this is the property of the Royal Duchy of Cornwall it is unlikely to be split up for sale and exploitation. Cornwall itself, of course, is also largely "Duchy", but, if Pembroke is to have coastal protection by way of "parking", Cornwall has an even greater claim for this kind of bulwark against bungaloid invasion and the litter of shacks and caravans so often defiling the sands and bays of our most attractive shores.

In England's middle-west there are two forests which are likely to become Forest Parks in the hands of the Forestry Commissioners. One is the Forest of Dean, the other the New Forest. As has been explained the Commissioners have already made a start in England and in Scotland. A National Forest Park has been defined as "an extensive Forestry Commission property in which the Commissioners have added to their planting activity the definite purpose of encouraging public access, more especially to the unplantable land, and of providing hostels, camp-sites and other facilities". It has to be remembered that a Forest Park cannot yield total access, as the risk of fire and of damage to young trees may be too great to allow of camping and hiking in much of its terrain.

The Midlands certainly need relief and Shropshire and the Malvern Hills suggest themselves as possible candidates. In East Anglia the Forestry Commissioners have big holdings and a Forest Park is possible round the planted areas of "Breckland". A Water Park, comprising the Broads, is another attractive possibility. The vast, clumsy sprawl of Greater London urgently needs a generous scheme of Green Belts. Territory for a National Park hardly suggests itself in this area, only perhaps in a scheme for cordoning off what is left of the South Downs. The coast of Kent and Sussex is now so nearly a continuous built-up area that, if anything can be done to keep the Downs as Belloc and Kipling knew and loved them, "So noble and so bare", it will be a blessing indeed.

The pattern of National Parks thus drawn is tentative. It is also elastic and in that resembles the pattern of the National Trust, which has been able to include several kinds of wardenship in its valuable watch over our rustic and architectural heritage. The Trust owns land directly: it holds protective covenants, which, while continuing private ownership, prevent sale for "development"; it also takes over, on request and with endowment, old and famous houses so that the public as well as the owners may have a share in their enjoyment. This scheme saves these mansions from becoming deserted, derelict, and ruinous or being put to uses never intended by their builders. A similar variety might mark the work of a National Parks Commission, which would have Parks under its own direction such as I have suggested, would co-operate with the Crown and with the Forestry Commissioners in creating and maintaining Forest Parks around the big plantation areas (the Ardgartan Park in Argyllshire is a Scottish model) and would do its share for coastal preservation by setting up, where possible, a series of cliff and beach

Parks (if that word can be used of strips of land beside the shore). It would also be interested in nature reserves, endeavouring to include these in "Park" areas.

British social policy will have to strike a balance between use of land for recreation and use for production. The supporters of National Parks, while approaching this problem from the recreation end, are well aware of this necessity. They believe that certain areas are naturally fertile in health and holiday pleasures, being most suited to refresh the senses, fill the lungs, and lift up the heart of the urban workers who are the vast majority of the population. These areas are rarely wholly barren; they have their hill-sheep, their woodlands, their dale-farms, their minerals, and all these sources of old wealth can be used as before and perhaps even better within the framework of a National Parks Commission, whose technical advisers on agriculture, silviculture and mineralogy would be at least as well equipped and as keen on their job as the guardians of looks and amenities. There is not the slightest reason why access to mountains and maintenance of landscape beauty should impede the old rural occupations and industries, if control be wise. The bringing of far more people to the country will eventually create problems of holiday housing and control of noise, litter and nuisance in general. These are problems with which the National Trust has already had to cope and its experience will be valuable if National Park Commissioners are in future to attempt the doubly urgent task of liberating land for popular use and controlling it to prevent popular misuse. They will be better able to do so in specifically scheduled areas than are the numbers of local authorities at present existing and often overlapping. They will have to face the great and ever-growing challenge from the cheapness and efficiency of mechanized transport, by air, land, and water. This transport is both the boon and the peril of a leisured democracy, since it frees the urban crowds from urban limitations and so inevitably menaces the neighbourhood of much-frequented beauty-spots. A National Park must never be just a national car-park, but it must not be controlled by the well-intentioned medievalists who shiver at the sight of a loaded motor-coach. We must work with the tools of our own time to promote the full fruition of nature's handiwork and man's. People will drive in plenty to the edge of the Parks, but not too freely through them. New motoring facilities in desolate places are the last thing wanted and instead of Sty Head Pass being given an "A" road (followed by Ye Old Gable Road House) it will remain its tremendous self, achievable only by taking effort. I conceive it is essential to all rural policy that there shall still be some places which you cannot reach or escape from by just ringing up a taxi, places only won by walking, climbing, and facing of hardship, even of risk. The National Parks, like the National Trust, will be stern guardians of this wilderness and its devotees, while no less generously providing the easier amenities for others who lack physique or inclination for the summits and cannot face the austerities and severities of a holiday spent wholly afoot.

II

COUNTRY AND COAST

By Harry Batsford, hon. a.r.i.b.a.

" The beauty of England, so easily fouled or broken in a tiny and thickly populated land, may be tender as a flower; we must be guardians of our garden."   the observer, 26th November, 1944.

At the height of the 1941 raid campaign an old friend wrote from Philadelphia, "Your cities are getting badly knocked about, but I am afraid that your lovely countryside is also getting largely spoilt." We replied, "It is beyond the power of the Germans to spoil the countryside by anything short of trampling over it by invasion. Besides, the English are spoiling the country very effectively themselves and need no enemy help; we will show you some excellent instances when you next come to England."

It is a curious paradox that to-day, when never before was the English countryside appreciated and visited by so many, the forces that make for its spoliation were never so manifold and so active. The proverbial Englishman's saying, "It's a fine day; let's go out and kill something", has been replaced by the fiat of an official body, "Here's a fine piece of land; let's put up something enormous on it." It seems that much that is mellow and lovely is doomed to be attacked and obliterated by a process as inevitable, as mechanical and as irresistible as the erosion that tears down our coastal cliffs, deepens river valleys and wears away the solid structure of the mountains themselves. So far the only permanently effective safeguard is to remove the threatened area from the action of this *Erosion of Civilization*, as we may call it.

Mr. G. M. Young, whom we all rejoice to welcome as one of the contributors to this volume, has declared "I have no great love for potted landscapes, and I shall join no society for Putting England Under a Glass Case." A tendency towards preciosity of preservation is certainly apparent in some recent Reports; it will never do to relegate the countryside to something approaching an Indian Reservation. Nevertheless, for all the mellow and matured beauty that surrounds us, I cannot help thinking of the words of the Prayer Book, "when we are set in the midst of so many and great dangers".

Ask yourself what would have been the state of many of the 110,000 or more acres now Trust-owned if they had been left undisturbed to their ordinary fate. When you see a fair Chiltern hillside messily disfigured by mean speculative building it may well be said, "There, but for the National Trust, goes Pentire Head, or Selworthy Glebe, or Marley Common or Ide Hill." The Trust owns something like a square mile in the fine Derbyshire Manifold Valley. It is now proposed to erect an extensive cement works there, and to convert the upper reaches of the valley into a reservoir for the Leicester Corporation, a suggestion characterized by a recent correspondent as "sheer vandalism".[1]

The fact is that the nation has, speaking generally, assumed no responsibility for the protection and preservation of its heritage, nor devised any machinery by which spoliation and desecration can be averted. The position is well summed up in a recent *Sunday Times* leader:

"Saving the threatened famous view of Lincoln Cathedral is a public gain which has cost the public nothing. But there are other gains in preserving the fast diminishing beauty of our land which cannot be made without cost. An instance is the appeal by the National Trust for the public preservation of Clumber Park. If the £40,000 still required for this pleasant stretch of 'the Dukeries' is not forthcoming we shall have failed in our duty.

"We use the words 'public duty' deliberately. The State—which is not some remote abstraction, but all of us—has for long embarked on a policy of taxation which is making it increasingly impossible for the families who for generations have preserved these oases of peace and beauty to do so any longer. Whether that is a good thing or a bad need not be argued here, though in passing we may deplore the growing tendency in some quarters to regard the possession of property, and especially of real estate, as in some way anti-social. The real charge against us as a community is that though engaged in expropriating the individual we make no effort to replace him in his role of preserver of the countryside.

"True 'the State' agreed to the foundation of the National Trust and empowered it to hold for the public good such portions of England as it may be lucky enough to secure. But 'the State' has never made any effort to endow the Trust with funds to carry out this laudable task. The ability of the Trust to do so still depends on the individual will to support it with hard cash. That is why it is a public duty not to let slip such opportunity as this."

(Just on going to press it is announced that the required sum has been subscribed.)

It does not look as if the present age is capable of creating beauty, but there is no doubt of its ability to obliterate and destroy what has come down to us from earlier times; it is only necessary to think of what loads have been placed on the long-suffering face of our land between the two wars to realize something of the desperately unfortunate tendency which is ceaselessly at work. Nevertheless we need not seek to evoke the nostalgic vision of a vanished and irrevocable past—the population is bound to increase, for some little time at least; people must have somewhere to live, so that building on the outskirts of great cities is bound to continue, though the conception of a Green Belt surrounding them is wise and far-sighted: things cannot be left to take their course unchecked. The idea of "dispersal" has also benefits, material, psychological and strategic, but a recent study published under that title would seem to show that the idea is likely to founder on the determined opposition of the staffs concerned. Let us assume that you own a pleasant, moderate-sized hilltop estate, which

---

[1] Later: the cement works is to be permitted, under the supervision of the Ministry of Town and Country Planning. Everything is to be carried out in an "orderly" sequence, "to the satisfaction of the Minister". It remains to be seen whether it will be to anyone else's satisfaction.

you prize for its splendid view, with several compact farms which have been well let. All you ask is that you may be left in undisturbed enjoyment of your little piece of England and its prospects. But the War Office wants to take the place for tank manœuvring and artillery observation; the Admiralty are after it for a compass-testing station and a wireless experimental centre; the R.A.F. think it is just the thing for a glider landing ground, or flying-bomb launching site. The Forestry Commission regard it as an ideal spot for adding to the acreage of its legions of regimented conifers; a large town wishes to lay out a huge housing estate on the top, a still bigger and more distant city wishes to construct a reservoir on the estate, and a county council plans to set down a super-splendid madhouse, which it has been the hobby of county councils to erect between the wars—and they always put the beastly things on the highest hilltop for miles around, possibly to cheer the inhabitants by the sight of their future residence; presumably now this war is over, they will be avid to put up enormous institutions for T.B. and V.D. If only all these bodies would cancel each other out they might achieve the result of the Kilkenny cats; as it is, you find yourself enmeshed in many "separate and distinct damnations, one sure if t'other fails".

But let us turn from anxieties to achievements.

Reviewing the position in this year of its jubilee, what has the National Trust managed to garner of the English scene as a result of fifty years' work? In a recent report Lord Zetland hoped that by its jubilee the Trust would be the owner of 100,000 acres of English countryside; with the increasing rate of accretions this figure has already been well exceeded. Subject to its wise and inevitable conditions of acceptance the National Trust may be reckoned fairly omnivorous. It does not despise the day of small things. It can, and does, accept and care for with equal alacrity a half-acre field and an estate of ten square miles. The result of this policy is that it has garnered in something, and in most cases quite a lot, of everything worth having, and has in its possession a fine balance, a harmony and diversity in which all worth while is well brought together.

In the Trust country, therefore, is found beyond doubt an excellent cross-section of the English landscape in all its types and varieties; there is none which is unrepresented. It owns the highest mountain peak in England, and the last original stretches of dead flat fen; in its list famous beauty spots thronged by tourist-queues alternate with little-known places where no one ever goes, and parks of sophisticated refinement contrast with rugged wild moors and fells. It possesses the highest spots in certainly six counties, and quite possibly in others.

The number of important historic country estates in Trust hands has recently shown a remarkable increase, in response to the special scheme initiated by them. It must be borne in mind, however, that at any given moment there is bound to be a number of country house estates where negotiations are not completed, so that though they will undoubtedly join the company, it is not possible to mention their names. There are also estates which have been willed to the Trust, but these cannot yet be included, for they remain in present ownership till the will becomes operative.

As distinctive and delightful as the country which the Trust has pieced into a mosaic covering England and Wales are the names which many of the places bear, a number of them doubtless since very ancient times. We do not sufficiently explore and enjoy our place-names, not only of the towns and villages which any gazetteer spreads before us, but those of farms and woods and hills and brooks and fields and commons and headlands. At a Corona-tion it was a joy to read the musical names of the heights where beacons were to be lit, and there are folk who abhor the sport yet never miss the hunting accounts in *The Times* for the sheer joy of the names of the meet and the little intimate places of the course. Doubtless when paper is once more in normal supply, if ever in our lifetime, the Trust annual report will print a fuller list of places than ever, with all its newest additions. The list is a joy, and it will be worth hunting some of them up, though it is well to be prepared for dis-appointment; there are some Dorset villages with heavenly names where a visit means grievous disillusionment.

Here are a random few from the great store of Trust places, and it is a pleasant exercise to see of how many it is possible to trace the locality without looking them up: Adventurer's Fen, Angrouse Cliff, Blackbottle Rock, Bordrigg's Brow, Broadbarrow Green, Coneysburrow Cove, Croaker's Patch, Emerald Bank, Exceat Saltings, Frydinghurst Common, Grexy Combe, Hanging Isley, Horne's Ride, Iron Tors, Lisnabreeny, Nancy's Rock, Nightingale Valley, Nutscale Combe, Old Man of Mow, Pencobben, Pennywilgie Point, Piggle Dene, Pinfarthing, Pollock's Path, Predannack Wartha, Prickly Pear Blossom Park, Rampsholme, Reskajeage Downs, Robin Hood's Arbour, St. Justinian's, Shadybank Common, Shining Cliff Wood, Six Brothers' Field, Slack Orchard, Sweetworthy Valley, Taw House and Wha House, Tilber-thwaite, Tregenna and Caragloose, Twelve Apostles, Wallowbarrow Crag, Wheal Emily, White Moss Intake, Wilmersham, Ynys Gwelltog.

Incidentally it is not the Trust's job to arrange to pillory some spots as "awful examples", perpetual warning of the results of thorough-paced spolia-tion, after the fashion of those "museums of horror" on the Continent. The idea, however, is worth considering, though the local inhabitants would doubtless protest fiercely at being thus stigmatized. The number of places which would definitely qualify for inclusion is, alas, infinite, and it is rapidly increasing. Let us refrain from invidious mention. Planners of a rabid type might be ordered a compulsory tour of the most outstanding examples.

It was not suggested that I should deal with Borthwood Copse, Isle of Wight—but I rejoiced to see this old friend in safe keeping, for as a very small boy I used often to be taken by an almost blind grandfather for the walk from Lake hamlet along the path which bisects the wood's pleasant oaks and hazel undergrowth, across the fields to quiet little Newchurch. So the first little bit of real country with which I was made acquainted is now in Trust hands.

It is immensely valuable that the Trust has been enabled to preserve many areas, some of them of great extent, close to huge manufacturing districts. The blessing of this free access to open unspoiled country to the present and future inhabitants of chains of great and often grim cities is incalculable. The outstanding instance of this is found in the vast cluster of Trust-owned

Derbyshire properties, hill, moorland, valley and wood, strategically placed between the "conurbations" of Manchester, Crewe and the Potteries to the west, and Sheffield, Chesterfield and Derby on the east. But there is also a sizeable group round Birmingham, and a smaller one on the Wirral near Liverpool, though for that matter Manchester and Merseyside make their playground in Lakeland as well. As for London, it is by no means uncatered for, though as befits an area far vaster than all, the green spots lie round an irregular arc at a correspondingly greater distance from its centre—Chiltern woods, precious spaces near Maidenhead, and the arrays of fine sandy heaths, commons and copses round Hindhead, with a compact company of high-lying stretches in the North Downs, always with superb viewpoints over the Weald, which are shared by the spots on the Kentish sandy forest ridge centred on Westerham. These southern places are all in districts of high natural attractiveness, within easy reach of London, and hence specially liable to be engulfed by building. The conserving of even an acre in such endangered parts therefore ought perhaps to rank higher than the dedication of a square mile in some entirely rural area. We may well be glad that 88 acres of Pett's Wood, Orpington, has been acquired, including the memorial to William Willett, originator of Summer Time. This will serve as a "lung" to the people living nearby on estates of such extent that a special station has been opened for them on the Southern Railway main line. The two acres of Marley Heights above Kingsley Green near Haslemere are very precious, for themselves, of course, and because so many villas have arisen on the Edge around; it is a blessing that 163 acres of Marley Common and Wood have been bought or given to the Trust; the deplorable hamlet of Camelsdale just below shows how injudicious building can mar. To round things off, let us hope that the isolated sandy whaleback of Henley Hill to the south, with its unique position and views, may find its way into safe hands, to make the point of the triangle with Hindhead and Black Down. The incomparable wooded range of the South Downs a little farther south has also a clamant need for safeguarding; there are sometimes disquieting rumours as to its fate.

In briefly reviewing this 170 or more square miles acquired, it has been thought advisable and convenient to adopt a grouping under different types of country, rather than topographically—thus: Hills and Mountains; Moor and Fell; Downland and Wolds; Coastlands; Heath, Commons and their Copses; Woodland and Forest; Parks and Estates; and ordinary Farming Country, according to the method followed in two recent books: *The English Countryside* and *The English Countryman*. This arrangement is far from perfect, and may be impatiently dismissed as absurd, for the varied English country declines to let itself be thus rigidly classified; it rightly despises and objects to mere human ticketing and docketing, and exalts in overlapping and combinations—Heaths and Commons rise to quite high hills, which also naturally form much of Moor and Fell; all these will also include wide woodlands; Parks, too, take in woodlands and ordinary Farming Country and so on. For that matter it is a regrettable divorce to have to adopt the division of this book's chapters, to deal separately with the house and its park, the village or cottages and their surround-

4

ing land. But it cannot be helped; there have to be classified divisions if you are to avoid a confused jumble; neither words nor paint can set down the opulent unity of nature.

1. HILLS AND MOUNTAINS. (See also Moor and Fell, with which it is closely intertwined.) An interesting, varied, widely scattered group, which includes part of the west cliffs of the Cheddar Gorge, and two geologically akin spots over 1,000 feet at Eccles Pike and South Ridge Farm near Buxton. Covenants also protect 1,036 acres of the north-western Welsh border Clwydian Range, near Moel Fammau, rising to 1,500 feet. The only representa-tive of the mid-Welsh border highlands is half a square mile of the 1,284-ft. Bradnor Hill, north-west of Kington. It towers above road and rail and looks at Radnor Forest and the Wye. It is to be hoped that more of these Shropshire hogbacks will be brought into the same fold. (The Abergavenny twins, farther south, come later.) But on the inner edge of this country there is covenant protection over most of the wooded Southern Malverns, less high but more interesting scenically and geologically than the northern portion, and neither so inhabited nor so accessible. Midsummer Hill is in its ownership, and covenants cover over two square miles, with nearly all the ridge from above Little Malvern to Chase End Hill, the 800-ft. last peak, including below the wide open expanse of Castlemorton Common, just now under wartime plough. The rest of the Malverns have their own conservators, but owing to mercenary obstinacy in the past the hills have suffered from extensive quarrying, which the urge of war needs has raised to full pressure. Working for six years on the slopes, I hear the blast of charges tearing away the plutonic rocks, to be sent off crushed in lorries for road material. There are two huge quarries on the Trust portion; it is hoped that all these baleful activities will be made to cease, even if it requires a special Act. From the Malverns, prominent on the south-eastern horizon is the gently curving, flattened dome of May Hill with a tiny tuft of trees. It is made of hard yellowish sandstone of a special kind, and is just under 1,000 feet. It is nearly all the Trust's, but an inscription testifies to an earlier local effort to preserve a part; in June last year this bore in yellow chalk the name of a gentleman from Tuskegee, Alabama. Its name is said to com-memorate the annual visit of local youths for spring dances. The view is completely circular, and inexpressibly noble and varied; perhaps its finest feature is the winding, ever widening silvery course of the lower Severn, here incipiently estuarial. The dominating strategic position of May Hill and its superb observation make it an incomparable key point, and had Hitler brought off his projected incursion up the Severn, it would have been the scene of desperate and prolonged fighting. From it, looking due westward, two sharp peaks stand out from the welter of hill ridges. They are the Sugar Loaf and Skirrid Fawr, both near Abergavenny and both belonging to the Trust; they are old red sandstone, southern outliers of the diamond-shaped Black Mountain massif. The Sugar Loaf, in Welsh Mynydd Pen-y-Fâl, shows from most aspects a graceful shapely cone; though it stands far back, its 1,955-ft. summit commands a vast expanse, and is visible from above Ludlow nearly 40 miles off. Owned or protected, the Trust has in keeping just four square miles of its area.

7   The Sugar Loaf and the Usk, near Abergavenny, Monmouthshire

8   Skirrid Fawr, or the Holy Mountain, near Abergavenny, Monmouthshire

9 Derwentwater and Skiddaw in Winter

10 Troutbeck Park Farm in the Lake District

Across the valley, Skirrid Fawr shows a sloping ridge, or end on a sharp peak of 1,596 feet; these dramatic changes of shape recall Suilven in far north-west Scotland, though lower and less drastic. Its legend of an earthquake on the day of the crucifixion rendered it intensely sacred to the Welsh, who would take sackloads of the soil to scatter over their pigsties, stables and even farm-house floors to avert the evil eye. The little St. Michael's chapel formerly near the summit was a place of medieval pilgrimage. A recent acquisition is 27 acres of the summit (894 feet) of the Dorset Lewesdon Hill near Beaminster on the rim of the northern ridge dominating Marshwood Vale, with its slightly higher neighbour Pilsdon Pen forming the twin highest points in Dorset. Birmingham open spaces are enriched by the Cadbury gift of Frankley Beeches, a hilltop of 829 feet with a conspicuous clump, on the city side of the Clent Hills above Rubery. Dunkery Beacon will be found mentioned in the *Moor and Fell* section.

Highest, noblest and most extensive of the Trust hill reservations are its ownings in the Lake District, which are constantly receiving additions. These lands include much in every one of our scenic divisions except Fens and Levels. Even if there is much Fell and Moorland, a brief review is perhaps most convenient here, though a full chapter would not do justice to its holdings, which could well take a small book. There are just one hundred places on the list, comprising 17,000 acres owned and 17,700 protected, that is about 54 square miles in all. It is already in itself a National Park in miniature, and it is earnestly to be hoped that on the Trust portions and throughout strenuous efforts will be forthcoming to remove the ravaging disfiguring scars of wartime occupation.[1] In a wide arc round Wasdale lie two great areas, now united by Seathwaite Farm, much of it dedicated as a 1914 war memorial by the Fell and Rock-climbing Club. There is also protection over land by Wastwater and farther below. Scafell Pike, 3,210 feet, the highest point in England proper, was given by Lord Leconfield as a Lakeland war memorial; there are also Scafell itself, 3,162 feet, and Great End, 2,984 feet, Allen Crags and others. On the other side are Great Gable, Green Gable, Kirkfell, among other favourite climbing peaks, overlooking the long winding stretch of high-lying Ennerdale with the River Liza twisting down to quietly lovely Ennerdale Water. Here the Forestry Commission has protected 5½ square miles stretching each side of Ennerdale, with Steeple and Pillar, across to High Stile. Now we are directly over Buttermere, which with its twin Crummock Water is Trust-owned, together with pleasant little Loweswater, and, leading from Buttermere, two miles of Honister Hause, steeply rising between high sharp crags. Down past the Hause the road drops into rugged charming Borrowdale, where Wordsworth would rejoice that the Trust has the Birches, the Bowder stone, Grange Fell and Castle Crag. We are now almost at Derwentwater, where the Trust has a chain of places along the south-west and north-west shores, including many exquisite viewpoints, much fine woodland under Cat Bells, with Friar's

---

[1] This pious hope seems to be doomed to a very scanty fulfilment, equally uncertain and remote The obnoxious Government Bill, just out of consideration in Committee, does not seem able to escape a liability to grave objection, a fundamental wrongness of principle—that of evading compensation by retaining property requisitioned for the duration only.

Crag and Lord's Island. There are also protected places in the Vale of Newlands.

South of Scafell the Trust has taken over parts of the two charming secluded valleys of Eskdale and Duddon; both are particularly liable to attract the speculative builder. In Eskdale there are Taw House and Wha House, and Penny Hill Farm; in the Duddon valley, Wallowbarrow Crag and 1,215 acres at Dale Head. Adjoining are the four square miles of the Monk Coniston estate, making a continuous wide belt across the Furness Fells, with the two 2,500-ft. heights of Wetherlam and Broad Slack. Included are the delightful lakelet of Tarn Hows, and land at each end of Coniston Water. Islanded to the north are the Trust Langdale lands and farms; by which, owing to Doctor Trevelyan's generosity, the splendid valley is well protected. There are many small properties at Ambleside, by Grasmere, and round Windermere, with fine views of the Lake. The list of farms, estates and woods round Hawkshead is extensive, so that the Trust is amply represented in Lancashire Lakeland. Under the Heelis Bequest, by which so much farm and woodland acreage has been conveyed round Coniston and Hawkshead, the Trust assumes the ownership of Troutbeck Park Farm near the Kirkstone Pass, three square miles of fell grazing, with some of the High Street Roman road and numerous remains of ancient settlements. As in Beatrix Potter's lifetime, hare and otter hunting are to be prohibited.

To the east, covenants have been secured over a square mile of land on two farms, Till's Hole and Stockdale Farm, in Longsleddale. It is pleasant to think that the head of this typical and almost unknown valley is now safeguarded; it is a bright little place, dotted with farms and cottages. Finally there is the splendid group at the western end of Ullswater, with Gowbarrow Park, including Stybarrow Crag and Aira Force waterfall, and restrictions over Glencoyne Park.

2. MOOR AND FELL. There are moorland stretches to be considered in Lancashire, Yorkshire, Northumberland, North Wales, as well as moorland in estates in Central Wales and Northumberland, which will come under *Parks*. But the main bulk of the Trust lands of this type, after the large Lakeland group already treated, is in the Pennine country and on Exmoor. In Derbyshire and Staffordshire the Trust places are scattered over a wide area, and fall into several groups. They include all features characteristic of Pennine scenery —acres of open rolling moorland, capped by dramatic tree clumps and threaded by seams of drystone walling, dropping by steep rounded shoulders down to winding river valleys beneath, stretches of vast woodland clothing the steep hillsides with a shaggy covering, limestone scar-faces and rock-spires rising almost from the river banks. It is an achievement that there is a group of extensive farms in Edale, with all its startling changes of aspect, from Edale Head right under the Peak to Edale End and beyond. Recent outstanding additions are Mam Tor, "the Shivering Mountain", with its remarkable banded strata, and the Winnats, that strange impressive pass of towering limestone sides. Further down in the Derwent valley below Hathersage is the extensive Longshaw estate and the broken Froggatt woodlands. There is a

triangular piece of Miller's Dale at its confluence with Tideswell Dale, and 49 acres of the fine hilly stretches of Taddington Wood, by Demons and Monsal Dales. But the main Trust country is around Dovedale, stretching for miles along each side of the lovely valley and including Ilam rock and the towering spires of the Twelve Apostles, capped on the north by the great stone dome of Wolfscote Hill. It is a consolation that some of the fine Manifold valley—as we have seen, so gravely and so doubly threatened—is Trust-protected to an increasing extent—from Wetton and Ossum's hills down to the parklands of Ilam Hall.

Altogether there are some 7 square miles owned and 5 protected in the Peak, well distributed, in a district which has witnessed the most recent grim and embittered skirmishes between the owners' keepers and the public determined to ramble over it.

The Exmoor lands belonging to the Trust include much of its eastern edge overlooking the vale of Porlock. By the generosity of Sir Richard Acland in transferring the whole of the Holnicote estate, the Trust has secured a further 20 square miles of this incomparable country; its properties include the gently swelling breast of Dunkery Beacon with vast and glorious views; its 1,707 feet is the highest point in Somerset. The estate also includes the wooded Horner valley, and the villages of Selworthy, Bossington, Allerford and Luccombe, and much of Selworthy Beacon and Bossington Hill, with over a mile of the cliffs; thus building can be stopped from spreading from Minehead's North Hill. The islanded 38 acres of Selworthy Glebe have been purchased as well; they were already "zoned for building development". Also in Exmoor, some miles due south, the Trust has two square miles of Winsford Hill's whale-back, rising to 1,405 feet above the Barle. On the broken western edge of Dartmoor there has lately come into Trust hands part of the fine Lydford Gorge on the Lyd, up to the waterfall, a favourite tourist beauty-spot.

In Yorkshire the Trust has Scarth Wood Moor near the Cleveland Hills, and some 400 acres between Whitby and Pickering, including the Bridestones Moor with its strangely shaped masses of rock. In East Lancashire the gift has been accepted of 433 acres in the Helmshore district; its moorlands and the cloughs leading to them are very popular with a large working population; equally acceptable are the 14 acres of moorland ravine at Medlock Vale, including the half-timber Hen Cote Cottage, Daisy Nook; they are a favourite resort of folk from the Manchester satellite towns. In Northumberland the acquisition of Hotbank Farm means that there are in Trust keeping some 1,200 acres of the wild high-lying moorland surrounding Hadrian's Wall, as it follows the course of the Great Whin Sill.

3. DOWNLAND AND WOLD. The first of these is very strongly represented, as is right—Chilterns, the North and South Downs, the Isle of Wight, Hampshire, Wiltshire and Dorset. Coombe Hill above Wendover is an outstanding landmark, and its 852 feet is the highest point of the Chiltern range. Its Boer War obelisk is visible from afar, and the vast prospect over the Vale of Aylesbury is shared by the 100 acres of Watlington Hill farther along the escarpment. Even the 5 acres owned and 58 protected on Whiteleaf Hill

below the chalk-cut Cross are valuable because of the suburbanization already spreading along its foot. The well-known and tourist-thronged Ivinghoe Beacon and Dunstable Downs farther north may be considered as a Chiltern extension, as is also Berkhamstead Common and Ashridge, mentioned else-where. One of the most recent covenanted areas in the Chilterns is also the most extensive—Lord Hambleden, in granting restricting covenants over 4,500 acres of the Greenlands estate, Henley-on-Thames, has protected for the public the rural character of a large part of the Hambleden valley, probably the most attractive in the Chilterns. The estate has also a considerable area on the Berkshire side, and includes three old country houses. Hambleden village lies a little back from the Thames, and what is rare among these hills, a bright clear stream flows for four or five miles from the north. The valley is wide, with beech-covered hills rising sharply on both sides, and at its head are great woods and a bold cluster of high downs above and around the twin villages of Fingest and Turville. The district was the site of several Roman villas, and the Hambledens have built a little museum for the excavated remains of their life and work. Hogback Wood, Beaconsfield, secures thirteen acres of beech and holly in a district which has been extensively built over during the last few decades.

On the North Downs, Box Hill, with Mickleham Downs, is of course a commanding viewpoint of unequalled popularity; the Trust has to foot a fairly heavy bill for collecting the litter into sacks after Bank Holidays. The little thirteen-acre piece of Hackhurst Down above Gomshall is an attractive hawthorn and sloe-dotted hillside, commanding fine southward views, together with the larger Netley Park nearby. Eastward along the escarpment the expanse of the Weald from Reigate and Colley Hills is equally grand and panoramic. On the South Downs the Trust keeps tree-fringed Newtimber Hill above Poynings, a jutting salient looking over the Weald to Cuckfield and the forest country, Highdown Hill on the seaward foothills near Worthing, and Cissbury Ring, described under *Ancient Sites*. The large Crowlink estate west of Eastbourne is a piece of downland by the sea, and includes two of the Seven Sisters cliffs. The Trust's two stakes in the western wooded South Downs are the extensive 1,050-acre Drover's estate near Singleton, on the forested southern slopes of the high main ridge, and the still larger Shoreham Gap property. In the Isle of Wight the Trust downland forms two pieces of very similar shape: $1\frac{1}{2}$ miles of the wall-like green height of St. Boniface Down, above Ventnor, and $1\frac{1}{2}$ miles of Highdown Cliffs, facing south in Freshwater Bay. Old Gilbert White would be glad that much of Selborne Hill and Common is now the Trust's, and part of his home estate is protected. On Salisbury Plain the Trust has two pieces of Pepperbox Hill, really the western end of Dean Hill, the chalk whaleback which, somewhat strangely, closes in the New Forest country to the north. There is control also over more than two square miles of pastureland, rich in prehistoric remains, surrounding Stonehenge, bought by public subscription to preserve from vulgarization the surroundings of the monument, which is itself cared for by the Ministry of Works. Finally, and most westerly, is Win Green, at 911 feet the highest

11   Mill Dale, Derbyshire: Viator's Bridge

12   Dovedale, Derbyshire: Iron Tors

13, 14
Win Green Hill
and its Clump of
Beeches, Cran-
borne Chase,
Wessex

15   Old Park Hill, Manifold Valley, Staffordshire

point of Cranborne Chase, and, I should think, of all Wiltshire downland. The windswept circle of beeches, visible from many a far mile away, is the culminating spot of a down landscape of noble impressiveness. The escarp‑ ment curves away on each hand, threaded by the Ox Drove Ridgeway, eastward to the northern projection of Winkelbury Camp, jutting out into an emerald‑ green landscape of fields and farms and hamlets, backed by a welter of long, ever‑greying distant ridges. At your feet the close downland turf drops steeply to a complex of deep‑curving combes, wooded or bare, and the eye ranges southward over leagues of lower stretches, broken here and there by little heights, to the faint grey line of the Purbeck Hills, and, if air and light be kind, the Isle of Wight itself. There is something majestically elemental in the sudden yet subtle sweep of the mighty hillside curves, and it seems entirely appropriate that this should have been the scene of the activities of many races of primitive man. Here General Pitt‑Rivers elaborated the technique of modern archaeo‑ logical excavation; he rests in the little church of Tollard Royal not far distant, and some results of his labours are preserved in the pleasant museum of human culture which he built nearby at Farnham.

By comparison the Trust holdings in the Cotswolds, 1,250 acres owned and 108 protected, seem modest, but they are all splendidly placed. There is Crickley Hill on the main escarpment near Birdlip, with a camp, like so much else bought and presented by the late Sir Philip Stott of Stanton Court, Broadway. South‑west of Painswick the Trust has most of the irregular projecting wooded hill‑piece which ends abruptly, high above twin rails and road, in the 787‑ft. camp of Haresfield Beacon, with a tremendous view over the widening Severn estuary to the Forest of Dean heights, backed by the Black Mountains. South of Stroud the Trust has obtained a mosaic of pieces of land on Rodborough and Minchinhampton Commons, which give it virtual control over a large tongue of high‑lying country between the Stroudwater valley and the Woodchester valley as far as Nailsworth. They are very uplift‑ ing, these wide, breezy stretches of upland common, up whose steep sides stone houses are irregularly dotted, while through sweeps of woodland the eye ranges over denser settlements dotted thickly along the valley far below.

4. COASTLANDS. Undoubtedly a greater area of coast has been encroached on and vandalized between the two wars than anything else except big town outskirts; hence the steadily mounting list of Trust seaside properties represents a real and vital safeguarding, and this specially applies to Cornwall. There is neither need nor space to give a full list of all the Trust‑owned stretches there, with the lovely strange‑sounding Celtic names: there are long ranges of splin‑ tered rocky cliffs, far projecting headlands, little sandy coves and wider bays. Among them are Chapel Cliff, Polperro; The Dodman and Nare Head, the two horns of Veryan Bay; Rosemullion Head and Trewarnevas Cliff each side of the Helford River, the granite Lizard Downs and Mayon and Trevescan Cliffs by Land's End. On the north coast are the great stretch from Godrevy and Navax points to Reskajeage Downs, the whole of Pentire Head and much cliff round Tintagel. Farther on in Devon there is East Titchberry Farm at Hartland Point, and an acre of Mount Pleasant, Clovelly. The little piece of

Kipling Tors by Westward Ho, if unspectacular and grandiosely named, will have an appeal for those who recall *Stalky*. The bold black wicked snout of Morte Point is balanced by Baggy Point across Morte Bay. The large area of hill and cliff east of Porlock Bay has already been mentioned. Elsewhere we may think of the covenant-protected lias headland of Golden Cap, Bridport, and by contrast of some meadows by Sidmouth and the quiet flatter areas of the Hampshire Hamble River. The Downland coast stretches in Sussex and the Isle of Wight have come in the previous section.

The six-mile piece of coast between Bolt Head and Bolt Tail (900 acres) which the Trust owns on the extreme southern tip of the Devon "Hams", is a high and impressive range, if not without its bleakness. The tall headlands of almost black rock plunge to the sea at an angle of 45 degrees. It is quite an experience to walk up from Hope Cove to the lookout station at dusk when the Eddystone starts to flash its beams around, and see the lights of the up-Channel shipping; the watcher will tell you right off that the three lights on a darker blur mean a Dutch cargo boat bound for Rotterdam. The line is broken by several little bays such as Starehole Cove; some are named after past sea tragedies, such as Ramillies Cove, where a frigate was wrecked in 1760 with the loss of 708 out of 734. Bolt Tail juts out beyond the little thatched fishing hamlet of Hope Cove, forming the eastern horn of Bigbury Bay. Here, long ago, the homeward-bound West Indiaman *Cantaloupe* ran ashore with the loss of all aboard. But as recently as April, 1936, the Finnish sailing ship *Herzogin Cecilie* went aground near Bolt Head in a fog, and in spite of all efforts to salve her, she was too firmly fixed on the rocks, so this fine survival had to be stripped and abandoned to her inevitable fate. There are ancillary properties at Portlemouth Down to the east and Clematon Hill in Bigbury Bay.

Next to Cornwall, the Trust's coastlands are mostly in Pembrokeshire, and there is nothing to choose between the two for splendour. The Gower Peninsula properties include Thurba Head and Dean Buckland's famous Paviland Cave. Beyond Tenby is the fine bold jutting headland of Lydstep, with its precipitous gable and great jagged hollowed-out caverns. There are six sections on the north side of St. Bride's Bay, and the restrictive covenants cover 6½ square miles. On the southern horn of St. Bride's Bay there are two stretches of bold cliffs by Marloes Sands and High Point, but the rest are round about St. David's—first a long range of steep grand cliffs west of Newgale. There are pieces of Trust coast each side of little Solva inlet, and a long range to the west by Porth y Rhaw, all of fine precipitous cliffs, with another mile west of Porth Clais. At Wales' farthest west there is protection over hilly Ramsey Island across its sound, a little miniature of Welsh coastland, with steep bird-filled cliffs, tiny harbours, and the four islets of Ynys Gwelltog, Ynys Cantwr and two smaller still. Just to the north we come to the abrupt upthrust of Cambrian rock at Carn Llidi's 595 feet, highest for many miles around, overlooking the sweeping arc of Whitesand Bay. Here the white farms and cottages dotted over the bare downs give a sense of remoteness from the world, and if we curve slightly round the southern tip of Ireland, only the Bishops and Clerks rocks stand between them and America.

The vantage point of Dinas Oleu above Barmouth must be mentioned, as
it was the first property conveyed to the Trust, in 1895; it commands immense
views over the infinite distances of Cardigan Bay. The Trust has five little
pieces on the Wirral, mostly on the west side; of these we need only mention
Thurstaston Hill. They are valuable open spaces for Birkenhead, and though
not on the coast they may come in this section, because from their heathery old
red sandstone slopes the eye ranges over the four-mile Dee estuary to the high
undulating line of the Flintshire hills. In Norfolk, Scolt Head Island and
Blakeney Point are kept as nature reserves. In the north-east the Trust, as well
as Lindisfarne Castle on Holy Island, keeps as a nature reserve the score or so of
the Farne Islands, associated with Grace Darling, scattered and remote off the
Northumbrian coast, with their strange-sounding names: Knocklin End,
Glororum Shad, Knivestone, Swedman.

Because of its abundant bird life, the Calf of Man is also reckoned as a nature
reserve. This little island is just under a square mile, and is situated off the
south-west tip of the Isle of Man, from which it is separated by a narrow sound.
Its only buildings are two lighthouses, a farmhouse with its outbuildings,
and a ruined church. Bracken and heather cover the slopes, which rise to a
highest point of 360 feet. It is a unique vantage spot, almost geometrically
in the centre of the Irish Sea, from which it is possible to look across to the
Mourne Mountains in Ireland, the Scottish Galloway heights, the Lakeland
mountains, and Snowdonia. A short time ago the Trust advertised for a
couple of caretakers of the island; there are doubtless many who, fonder
of birds than of their fellow men, would regard it as the ideal place to
pass their days, supreme without interference in their little self-contained
domain.

5. WOODLAND AND FOREST. The home woodlands have of necessity
suffered severely during the war, and, never anything but a poorly forested
country, England will come out of it with badly depleted timber acreage. It
is well that a considerable area of forest country has been confided to the Trust's
keeping on a self-supporting basis; there will be the opportunity to tend and
cherish, and possibly extend, the woods. With the large preoccupation of the
Forestry Commission with quick-growing conifers, it is essential that everything
possible should be done to keep and increase the amount of woodland of
deciduous trees, which are as great a national asset as any natural product. The
Trust's stake in England's woods is varied and widely distributed, but it happens
that woods form part of almost every kind of country: hills, downs, moors,
estates, parks, heaths, so that they naturally fall for mention under those
divisions; a number indeed have already been referred to, e.g. in the Chilterns
Hogback Wood, Beaconsfield; Taddington Wood, Derbyshire, and the extensive plantations of the Holnicote estate in West Somerset (p. 17). In the far-
flung company are the beech woods of the chalk, miles of hillside oaks, groves
of birch, areas of fir and larch, lines of high-standing ashes, and their extent
and scattering must set problems for economic and beneficial management.
I do not know the total area of woods in Trust possession, but it must be
considerable if it were all reckoned up.

Let us glance at a few widely separated woodlands on the Trust list. The Ashridge group on the hills above Berkhamstead includes the great tall Frithsden Beeches, 173½ acres of them, with, among others, Old and Rail Copses, Cromer Wood and Sallow Copse. There is Shining Cliff Wood, rising for over a mile above the west bank of the Derbyshire Derwent, and the broken woodland, mixed with pasture, under Froggatt Edge, south of Hather-sage. In Cheshire, little Maggoty's Wood, at Gawsworth, is full of bluebells in spring; it contains the grave of Maggoty Johnson, a curious eighteenth-century character. Near the Suspension Bridge are Leigh Woods, at Clifton, with their fine oaks and grassy rides on both sides of the Avon, including Nightingale Valley and two prehistoric camps. These 150 open acres are of great value so near to Bristol, and so will be the 400 of woods and farmlands of the Failand estate, only a few miles westward, which are on a hillside rising to a 500-ft. ridge and overlooking the Severn estuary. Equally vital for outer London are the 88 acres of Pett's Wood between Chislehurst and Orpington, with their pillar sundial memorial to William Willett of Summer Time fame, surrounded by a densely-built estate. In the Wyre Forest district, half a square mile of Longdon and Withybed Woods has been covenant-protected. The Trust has recently acquired 40 acres of Lardon Chase, Streatley-on-Thames, which ranks as a pendant to Coombe End Farm, 500 feet high, north of Pangbourne above Hart's Lock Woods and in an admirable strategic position to command the Goring Gap. Not far away is The Chase, Woolton Hill, between Newbury and Highclere, with 150 acres of mixed woodland which is to be kept for a nature reserve. To jump from Thames to Swale—both possess their Richmonds—we find over two miles of steep woods on the south bank of the river by Hudswell, including Calf hall, Round Howe and Billy-bank Woods, with Redbrow by Hag Wood, the latter a spot loved by the painter Turner. Finally there is Hatfield Forest, Essex, just east of Bishop's Stortford, 1¼ square miles of rolling country with many radiating rides and a large lake. It was one of the Royal Forests of Essex, and formed a deer park from Tudor times till 1915.

6. FENS AND LEVELS. In this domain the Trust is privileged to control the only parts of Fenland remaining in their original state. There is just over a square mile of Wicken and Burwell Fens, including Adventurers' and St. Edmund's Fens. They are carefully guarded to preserve their plant, bird and insect life, the latter including some unique species. Visitors are not greatly encouraged, and must sign an undertaking to abide by the rules of admission. Nevertheless it is well that access is not too sternly withheld to this interesting and beautiful survival of a type of country which human enterprise and economic pressure have banished from the face of the land. The long straight waterline of Wicken Lode stretches along the Fen, with an occasional old boat moored at its bank. It parallels a blind track from the pleasant little plaster and thatch village of Wicken with its pond, only a step away. Up neighbouring lodes an antique paddle-steamer will come to cut the reeds, which rise as a solid back-ground to the pools, tall and graceful under the vast overarching Fen skyscape. But the glory of the place is in late spring, when the water-lilies flower yellow

16   The Cliffs near Bolt Tail, Devon, with the stranded *Herzogin Cecilie*

17   Barras Head on the North Cornish Coast

18   Aston Wood, Oxfordshire, on the Chiltern Escarpment

19   Frithsden Beeches, Ashridge Estate, Hertfordshire

and white among their massed heart-shaped rafts of leaves. As already mentioned, the Trust also possesses extensive levels in Norfolk at Blakeney Point and Scolt Head Island, which are nature reserves.

Among levels also may be reckoned the area of Runnymede meadows stretching for two miles along the Surrey bank of the Thames by Egham, and ever to be preserved for their associations, now of some 700 years' standing, with Magna Charta. Historical associations of another type are connected with the disused Royal Military Canal which begins at Hythe near Folkestone, and runs for many miles curving across Romney Marsh; of this the Trust owns the 3½ westerly miles from Appledore. It was cut in 1807 as a barrier against Napoleonic invasion, and it represents a feat of engineering, for the water-level is high above the low marshland, once covered by the sea. The canal is pleasantly shaded by trees, mostly wych-elms planted in close continuous rows to hold the banks together. In addition the Trust has 4½ acres of levels at Exceat near Seaford on the Cuckmere River in Sussex, with a small piece of the saltings themselves. And I like the spirit of the peer who, that all might be complete and every type of country represented, arranged for the Trust to acquire 60 acres of sand dunes on the Northumbrian coast near Bamburgh.

7. PARKS AND ESTATES. It is in this sector that the greatest increase of properties and acreage has come to the Trust in the last few years, and the list of important estates acquired or in process of negotiation is assuming very large proportions, and brings to the executive many problems of administration and finance. The Trust's Country House scheme is meeting with a slow but steady response. We are here concerned only with the estate lands, but Mr. Lees-Milne will have no difficulty in showing that the Trust's historic country houses can in themselves provide an outline history of domestic architecture and garden design. Some properties have already been noted in previous sections, and only brief mention can be made of some of the more outstanding places, which, as we have seen, in themselves epitomize the types of native landscape, and contain extensive forest tracts and wide stretches of admirable farming country. As might be expected, there are more parks in Trust hands in the south-eastern division than elsewhere. Ashridge has been already touched on, and high above a fine reach of the Thames are the hanging woods and grounds of Cliveden. Lord Astor's munificent endowment is the greatest in the history of the Trust, and it is his wish that the gift should be applied to promoting fellowship and goodwill among the English-speaking nations. Not far away the fine park of West Wycombe, seat of the Dashwoods for 250 years, stretches up the Chiltern slopes; it contains temples and a large lake, and its layout is the work of the famous landscape gardener Humphrey Repton. The Trust now has the triple ensemble of great house, park, and idyllic village at its foot. In the same county is Dorney Wood; here a gift of 200 acres of land will help materially to preserve the amenities of Burnham Beeches. In Surrey the gift of Polesden Lacey means the acquisition of a finely laid out park of exceptional attractiveness, across the Mole valley from Box Hill, hitherto inaccessible to the public. On the other side of the North Downs, Captain H. S. Goodhart Rendel's gift of Hatchlands, East Clandon, involves

421 acres of parkland, with a house containing much work of Robert Adam. "Batemans", Burwash, with its typical stone house, has associations with Kipling's later years, and slopes down to a stream in the pleasant hilly forest ridge country of East Sussex. Gatcombe Park, of 850 covenanted acres with church, lake and mid eighteenth century house, lies secluded in the exact centre of the Isle of Wight. In Wiltshire the recent acquisitions at Dinton have brought to the Trust 240 acres of hilly wooded land and three historic houses. Bristol's varied "lungs" include the 100 acres of Shirehampton Park over looking the widening Avon on the way to Avonmouth. In addition to the great Holnicote estate on the Exmoor borders, Sir Richard Acland has conveyed to the Trust his Killerton property north east from Exeter; this includes the village of Broad Clyst, about 4,500 farming acres and 1,000 of forest. The south side of the hill has been finely laid out with rare trees and flowering shrubs. In Wales the Trust has acquired two large estates of exceptional scenic impressiveness. With later additions, the Dolaucothi Estate, Pumpsaint, Carmarthenshire, extends over four square miles. It lies midway between Towy and Teifi in the midst of steep 1,000 ft. hills pointing roughly south west, and often densely wooded. Through the midst flows the river Cothi from its source in the bare hills beyond Tregaron, the largest uninhabited roadless wilderness south of the Highlands. The very rural little hamlet of Pumpsaint is on the estate, whose chief claim to "news" is that it includes the Ogofan gold mine, which was certainly worked quite recently. A gold mine is also found on the Dolmelynllyn estate north of Dolgelly, placed in a beautifully wooded valley on the Ffestiniog road, and extending its sheep grazing high up the slopes of the 2,000 ft. Y Garn. With it go two isolated sheep pastures on the still higher Y Llethr, on the range which includes Diphwys and the Rhinogs. Ilam Hall, Staffordshire, has been referred to with the Dovedale holdings; the modern house has been partly pulled down and is used as a youth hostel. Right across England to the east lies the large Blickling Hall estate near Aylsham in Norfolk, once connected with the Boleyns. There is a fine Jacobean house and gardens, and the park contains a large lake, a mausoleum and a nine hole golf course; there are also extensive farmlands. In south east Lincolnshire the Trust has recently been presented with Gunby Hall, Spilsby, in an estate of 1,500 acres. There is a Stuart house of distinction standing in a compact gently undulating park. Lastly there is the great Wallington estate in North umberland, with its 20 square miles of extent, probably the greatest single item in the Trust list; it is important not only for its mansion but as a place where northern city dwellers come, and will come still more, to ramble over the splendid spaces of its open moorlands. Part of the outbuildings have been used as a youth hostel; the park stands near Scot's Gap Junction in a lonely upland district of rolling fells and little streams, rising to the 1,500 ft. hills of Rothbury Forest.

8. HEATHS AND COMMONS. A section of many holdings, some very extensive, centred chiefly in the three south eastern counties, but also occurring in Hertfordshire and Berkshire, the Midlands and the East, though the Trust does not seem to possess any of the Breckland heath country on the Norfolk

Suffolk borders. To take the outlying places first, there are 1½ square miles of Berkhamstead Common, high-lying and well wooded, largely with birch, and a detached 116 acres of Hudnall Common. This was in the mid-nineteenth century fated for enclosure, and was only saved by the public-spirited action of a band of country-lovers, who chartered a special midnight train and brought down a posse of labourers with crowbars to tear down the barriers already illegally erected. Most of the commons acquired in Berkshire are scattered in an irregular oval round Maidenhead, from the Thames to the Bath road; they were bought by local residents, whose enterprise has thus secured a chain of wide open spaces for a densely-built residential district. From Winter Hill and Cock Marsh by a loop of the river there are wide views northward to the Chilterns.

The Trust has rights over Outney Common on a loop of the Waveney near Bungay, Suffolk, and in the Berkshire heath country portions of Ambarrow Hill and Finchampstead Ridges. Kinver Edge, near where three Midland counties meet, is a sharply-rising ridgelet of gorse, bracken and copses, with rocky outcrops, an early Iron Age camp, and some of the curious local inhabited rock-dwellings could supply tea. Its views over a wide extent of country render it a favourite spot with Midland city dwellers.

In the hillier north of the New Forest there is a continuous chain of commons covering 1½ square miles: Plaitford, Bramshaw, Cadnam and others, with several hamlet "greens". In Surrey the Trust has the richly wooded 447 acres of the Bookham commons between the station and the Mole, and a scattered group round Witley, including Hydon's Ball and Hydon Heath, which rises to a commanding position, 593 feet high, and was bought as a memorial to Octavia Hill. Far south across the Weald, in Lavington Common, Petworth, the Trust has a stake in the pleasant chain of low purple heather and pine-wooded commons along the western Rother near the South Downs escarpment. Most extensive of all, however, is the group of Hindhead commons, acquired piecemeal over a term of 32 years, a wise and public-spirited effort in view of the spate of late Victorian building at Hindhead. They total in all 1,775 acres or nearly three square miles, and the separate group south of Haslemere amounts to 686½ acres, over a square mile of Surrey, Sussex and Hampshire sandy forest country. All stand high, and are breezy expanses of gorse, heather and bracken with scattered fir trees dropping to wooded valleys; all overlook vast ranges of lower meadow country. Among them is the famous Devil's Punch Bowl and the great viewpoint of Gibbet Hill, and farthest north the curious rocky outcrops called the Devil's Jumps. Baring Gould's novel *The Broom Squire* has this district for its setting, and aims at depicting something of the curious characters who "squatted" in the Punch Bowl. The wide westward extension of Ludshott Common takes in the string of forested hammerponds known as Waggoners Wells. South of Haslemere the strategic importance of the Marley Common group has already been noted, and the recent acquisition of some 500 heather and pine-clad acres of Black Down makes the Trust owners of the highest point in Sussex, and with Leith Hill, of all the land over 900 feet in south-east England. From its sharp edge the immense view was thus described by Tennyson, who lived and died at Aldworth on the hill:

> . . . you saw the view
> Long known and loved by me
> Green Sussex fading into blue
> And one grey glimpse of sea.

We follow the broken sandy forest ridge north-eastward to Leith Hill, at 965 feet the highest point in south-east England. You can be over 1,000 feet by climbing to the top of the queer old tower and see thirteen counties, at a charge of twopence if you are misguided enough to be outside Trust member-ship. The most easterly group of Trust heath-pieces is outstanding, for they occupy dominant points in the densely-copsed Chart country south of Wester-ham and Sevenoaks—with two outlying viewpoints still farther east, One Tree Hill and Gover Hill. These are the trio of Toys Hill, Ide Hill and Mariners, on Crockham Hill, the only points in Kent over 700 feet. The immense panorama over the Weald is the same from all—the ground drops suddenly 300-400 feet, and a vast wooded green expanse spreads in front, widening and flattening to the eastward on your left hand. This is the wide corridor which forms the Eden-Medway valley, and across it the wooded heights of Ashdown Forest rise to form the southern horizon.

9. ORDINARY FARMING COUNTRY. It must be gratifying to the Trust executive that their stake in the country's agriculture is a large and growing one. I do not know the area of Trust land under cultivation or grazing, but it must extend over many square miles and include almost every kind of crop and farming. Much of it has come up for notice in the various other types of country, for farmlands are found almost everywhere. There are sheep farms square miles in area in Lakeland and on the Northumberland and Pennine moors, as well as smaller holdings on the chalk downs; farms on Cornish or Welsh coastal strips; farms amid forest country, and above all, productive holdings of crops and grass on estates great and small. The only division where agriculture is almost unrepresented seems to be in the Fens, most fertile and productive of all, but here the Trust is concerned with the pre-farming state, and does not hold a great area. Naturally there are little holdings found among the Trust Heath country, so execrated by Cobbett for its lack of farming qualities; certainly for the most part its return is from its woodlands and rough grazing, e.g. in Sussex copses the young sweet chestnut trees are cut at intervals and made into sheep hurdles on the spot. Actually 300 farming acres have later been added to Crockham Hill, to help preserve the view so dear to Octavia Hill. The two great gifts of Sir Richard Acland include many agricultural holdings—the Killerton estate at Broad Clyst comprises over seven square miles of farming land on the red Devon soil, and there are many Exmoor farms within the Holnicote boundaries. The Blickling estate in Norfolk has extensive farming tracts. Coombe End Farm, near Goring, was mentioned under *Estates*; the donor's widow continues to live there, and access is confined to the footpaths. In the Peak district in the long list of Trust places are, among others, Fulwood Holmes Farm, with Harrop Farm, in Edale; and, under covenants,

20   The Devil's Punch Bowl from the Surrey Heaths, near Hindhead

21   Black Down, Sussex, from Henley Hill

22 Dovers Hill and Chipping Campden, Gloucestershire

New Hanson Grange Farm in Dovedale. The names of the Lakeland Trust farms would take too long to quote; they are mostly both strange and musical. Several farming pieces have been given in the area surrounding Birmingham, but to some of them the public has no access. Restrictive covenants now apply to 717 acres of agricultural land surrounding Thorney Abbey House, Anglesey Abbey and Kirtling Tower, widely scattered in Cambridgeshire, the first two in the Fens, Thorney by Peterborough and Anglesey near Cambridge, while Kirtling lies comparatively high in the rolling chalklands. In Bedfordshire the Trust owns Roberts Farm and Sharpenhoe Clappers, the latter on a projecting spur of the chalk downs overlooking the plain to the north.

The Northern Ireland properties are a recent development, for they came to the Trust in 1937-8. There are 180 acres of chalk cliffs and sandy shore at White Park Bay on the North Antrim coast; there are two houses with grounds south of Belfast, a piece of wooded glen at Ballymoyer in Armagh, and an old earthwork, Rough Fort near Limavady, overlooking Lough Foyle. The only Trust property in Eire is Kanturk Castle, County Cork, which is practically confined to the building.

.   .   .   .   .   .

Even this scrappy, inadequate survey of what has been done should suffice to convince us all of the magnitude and helpfulness of the work accomplished, though it is inevitable that in more than one sense "there remaineth much land to be possessed". But let us thank God and take courage, even if there is still need to keep our powder dry; we can rejoice more than ever to-day that *Eppur si muove*. The trickle of the middle nineties has become a considerable spate; the graph of properties, of acres, square miles even, shoots upward with an ever steepening angle of ascent, an increasing excelsior. With all the latest available information to hand, it is inevitable that this record will be out of date before this book is published.

It is impossible for us to realize how much time and thought and care has gone towards this result, how much discussion, legal wrestling and tiresome intricate detailed negotiations; the debt to the Trust executive and staff is a heavy one. But let us also acknowledge gratefully the part played by the land-owning families in past and present. It is to their efforts that is due the creation of fine stretches of parkland, often of mellow farmlands, out of shaggy roughness; we are not here concerned with the enclosure question, but only with results. They often preserve effectively on their estates land near great cities which but for them would be pounced on as "ripe for building development". Now they are large-heartedly making over to the National Trust their estates and lands, often at decided personal sacrifice, and foregoing much gain by giving restrictive covenants on what could be profitably sold for building. Frequently, since the Trust can take over estates only on a self-supporting basis, the making over is accompanied by a munificent endowment.

Tribute must also be paid to the far-sighted enterprise of those who have brought desirable properties to the notice of the Trust, organized local subscriptions, and often themselves contributed handsomely. The donors by gift and will of funds, which are the indispensable sinews of war, must also be remembered thankfully. Everyone can help the cause by keeping watch for desirable proper, ties, lands or houses which are threatened with spoliation, lying derelict, or generally advantageous for preservation, bringing them to the notice of the Trust, and possibly later helping in the arrangements for taking them over. In this way much has been rescued which would have been lost.

But what of the future? None can tell what may be in store for Britain, save that there lurk many risks and difficulties in the mists of uncertainty looming ahead. One thing is clear, that in them the work and achievements of the Trust are destined to play an increasingly beneficial part for the healing of the nation. Is there the prospect of a trend towards planning and pressing us all into a soulless aggregation of urbanized helots? The love of the country is ingrained in the majority of the British race, and it is essential that they should have facilities to understand, explore and enjoy it. One great lesson of both the wars is writ large: we depend on the country and its workers for our very material existence. For six years they have cheerfully shouldered and carried through triumphantly a superhuman task. Let there be an end of meanly treating them as poor relations of city communities: "Except these abide in the ship ye cannot be saved". Equally vital is the part the country can and must play in the physical and spiritual refreshment and upbuilding of our people in the strenuous and difficult efforts that will be demanded of them. That is the firm conviction of all teachers and leaders who with vision and insight have the common weal at heart, as has been finely expressed in the significant words of Dr. G. M. Trevelyan:

"Without vision the people perish, and without natural beauty the English people will perish in the spiritual sense. In old days the English lived in the midst of Nature, subject to its influence at every hour. Thus inspired, our ancestors produced their great creations in religion, in song, and in the arts and crafts—common products of the whole people spiritually alive. To,day most of us are banished to the cities, not without deleterious effects on imagina, tion, inspiration and creative power. But some still live in the country, and some still come out on holidays to the country and drink in with the zest of a thirsty man the delights of natural beauty, and return to the town re,invigorated in soul."

23   Dunkery Beacon from Tivington Knowl, Somerset

24   The "Druids' Circle" beneath Saddleback, near Keswick, in the Lake District

III

ANCIENT SITES

By GRAHAME CLARK, F.S.A.

THE sites of prehistoric and Romano-British antiquity described in this chapter combine natural beauty with historic interest to an exceptional degree. Remote from modern industry, most of them are situated beyond the margin even of wartime agriculture. It is surely no freak of history that the Romantic Movement should have stimulated interest in British antiquities at the same time as it was discovering beauty in wild nature. The works of early man, ruined or at least smoothed by the hand of time, only improved the natural scene: the drama of Keats's "forlorn moor" was not diminished, but increased by that famous "cirque of Druid stones". As for ourselves, who has not thrilled at the sight of a burial mound or defensive earthwork, breaking the grim profile of a moor or dimpling and creasing the sinuous contours of a down? Who, again, contemplating the Wall, could easily dissociate Hadrian's triumph from its Border setting?

For the long ages of savagery, when our predecessors lived precarious lives, hunting, fishing and gathering for subsistence, we have few surviving traces other than tools and weapons made from flint and other durable materials. Extensive tracts of country were needed to support even small hunting bands, which roamed their territories, following the seasonal migrations of beasts and gathering the fruits of the earth as they ripened. Settlement was rarely fixed for more than a brief period and the huts and windbreaks, which for most of the year gave shelter to the hunters and their families, were of light construction, easily set up and as easily taken down. Among the few visible memorials of the men of the old stone age are the caves and overhanging rocks under which they passed the winter months. Both in Gower and in Cheddar Gorge, caves inhabited at this remote period are situated hard by lands of the National Trust. Paviland, famous as the finding place of the "Red Lady"—in reality the ochre-covered burial of a young man—lies between and close to the more easterly of two stretches of cliff owned by the Trust; a mile to the east, on National Trust land, the Long Hole, a narrow fissure in the Yellow Top Rocks, was also a resort of upper palaeolithic man. At Cheddar, the hunting bands, camping in the mouth of Gough's Cave on the east side of the gorge, must have looked out over what is now Trust property on the opposite side. Bones, antlers and teeth recovered from these caves show that the hunters pursued, among other victims, reindeer, bison and woolly rhinoceroses, denizens of territory held in the frozen grip of an Ice Age.

The transition to temperate conditions was marked by the withdrawal of ice-sheets, the incoming of forest vegetation and the separation of Britain from the continent. In the realm of human affairs no development of comparable magnitude supervened for long ages. For some further millenia savagery reigned over the land and small communities of gatherers continued their all-absorbing search for food, ignorant of the great economic changes which early began to unfold themselves in more favoured lands. The mesolithic (Middle Stone Age) tribes have left no more behind them than their palaeolithic predecessors, but their trail may often be picked up by locating spots where they flaked their flints, including the characteristic microliths or little pointed arrow barbs. Among other sites of this kind owned by the Trust may be cited Black Down, Haslemere, and Baggy Point and Pentire Head on the north coasts of Devon and Cornwall.

Our earliest archaeological monuments date from the time of the first spread of farming, and comprise camps formed by two or more concentric banks and ditches. The most famous of these is on Windmill Hill, Wiltshire, a low chalk eminence owned by the National Trust and overlooking Avebury from the north-west. The earthworks were never as strong as those of the later hill-forts and the progress of silting and denudation, operating over a period of between four and four and a half millenia, has so smoothed their profiles that from the ground it is often difficult to distinguish their plan. This applies with special force, where, as at Windmill Hill, a good proportion of the camp is under plough. The only way to get a really adequate impression of such a site is to fly over it, but failing that the best plan is to go first for the inner ring and then try and pick up the outer ones. From surface indications it is evident that the ditches are incomplete; excavation has shown them to be no more than irregular quarries. The banks formed of the excavated material can never have been sufficient to serve as defensive barriers in themselves. Most probably they held timber palisades. Entrances into the successive enclosures are indicated by unquarried causeways opposite gaps in the banks. The most likely explanation of such a site as Windmill Hill is that it served as a rallying place for communities largely dependent on herds.

Although they cultivated wheat and barley on a small scale, the economy of the Windmill Hill people was evidently based on mixed husbandry, in which pastoral activities were predominant. Large-horned cattle were the mainstay of the livestock, but pigs were also important. Dogs seem to have been common, but goats and goat-horned sheep were rare and horses non-existent. Technically the Windmill Hill people were neolithic; being without metal, they relied on flint and stone, both of which they had learnt to polish. Culturally their affiliations lay with Western Europe. The hand-made bowls, recalling leather prototypes in their forms and having little or no decoration, belong to a family widely distributed over a zone, defined on the north-east by the Rhineland and the Alps, and extending southwards over France, Iberia, the islands of the Western Mediterranean and North Africa as far east as the Nile.

The people of the neolithic camps, with which the closest analogies lie in certain camps of the Middle Rhineland, were only one of several immigrant groups to reach Britain from the Western neolithic province. Yet, thanks to the excavations at Windmill Hill and similar sites, we know more about this particular group than any other. As we stand on the low rampart of their camp and gaze away to the bold escarpment of Hackpen on the east or the course of Wansdyke on the skyline to the south over and beyond Avebury and Silbury, we may picture in our mind's eye those earliest farmers, venturing into a savage land, raising the first crops and gathering within the hilltop palisades the first herds to graze on British soil.

As time passed, the site was visited by other groups. Some, coming from the region extending from the Baltic to the Ukraine, made coarse pots with heavily impressed decoration; others made shapely beakers of a type ubiquitous in Western and Central Europe towards the end of neolithic times. All alike sought the best material for the axes needed to clear the densely forested land and to dress timber for houses and all manner of purposes. To satisfy this require-ment they were ready both to trade superior stone from afar and to mine the best flint from the parent chalk. At Cissbury, on the Sussex downs near Worthing, the National Trust owns a neolithic flint-mine second in importance only to Grimes Graves in Norfolk. All one can see to-day are the cup-shaped hollows defining the filled-in shafts, some two hundred of them within the western part of the Iron Age hill-fort and thirty-nine outside the southern entrance. Excavation has shown these shafts to be interconnected by a maze of subter-ranean galleries driven laterally along the flint seam. The ancients used stone axes and antler wedges and hammers to split the chalk, antler "picks" to lever it apart, and rakes and shovels to gather the rubble into baskets for hauling to the surface, the spoil from a newly-mined shaft being dumped into an abandoned one. To reduce freightage, the mined flint was dressed and the axe-blades roughed out around the mouths of the shafts.

At death some at least of our neolithic forebears could hope for burial in tombs of truly majestic proportions. Only those who have helped to excavate a Long Barrow can realize what the erection of such monuments must have meant to communities so scantily equipped and possessed of so slight a surplus of the necessities of life. Until we remember that the dead were regarded as much a part of the community as the living, it is hard to explain why so gigantic an effort was put forth without any obvious return. Long Barrows are of many breeds. Some have parallel sides, but most are wedge-shaped; some cover structures of timber and turf and others mask burial chambers built of great stone slabs in megalithic style. The "White Barrow" on National Trust property at Tilshead, Wiltshire, is an excellent specimen of a wedge-shaped earthern Long Barrow; some 255 feet in length and attaining to between 7 and 8 feet in height, it varies in width from 92 feet at its western to 156 feet at its eastern end. Of megalithic chambered Long Barrows the Trust can show two examples of widely differing character. The barrow at Randwick, Gloucester, is a degenerate specimen of a family introduced to the Cotswold-Severn region, most probably from Western France. The wedge-shaped mound, of which the western end had been quarried away, was origin-ally surrounded by dry-stone walling, which also reinforced the inner structure of the mound. At the broad eastern end of the mound is the small burial chamber, built of five great stone slabs. In this the excavators found hand-made pottery, flint flakes and "an extraordinarily confused mass of human bones". The Coldrum site, named after a farm in the parish of Trottescliff or Trosley, Kent, on the other hand, belongs to the small Medway Valley group, derived from the "Hunsbeds" of Denmark or Holland. The oblong chamber formed of massive slabs is placed near the eastern end of a rectangular stone setting. Excavation disclosed remains of no less than twenty-two individuals, comprising both sexes and all ages and exhibiting in their bony structure a certain family likeness. Both Randwick and Coldrum, then, were family tombs opened periodically to receive new bodies.

Easily the most picturesque of megalithic sites are the great stone circles, which first appeared under the stimulus of the Beaker invasions in the eighteenth or nineteenth century B.C. In the "Druids' Circle" at Keswick the National Trust possesses a beautifully placed example of the simplest type, comprising thirty-nine stones, set on a diameter of from 100 to 110 feet. Far more complex and on a much greater scale is the vast site in north Wiltshire, which includes the village of Avebury within a small portion of its enclosure. Since William Stukeley, more than 200 years ago, admired the "notorious grandeur of taste" with which it had been planned, the monument has been sadly mutilated by farmers who found the stones an impediment to tillage and a handy source of building material. Yet, thanks in part to the measure of scientific restoration carried out shortly before the site was acquired by the Trust, "the boldness of the imagination" which conceived it can still excite our admiration. The most arresting feature of the site is the great circular bank with its inner ditch. It was some 4,440 feet in circumference and the crest of the bank must originally have been fully 50 feet in vertical height from the bottom of the ditch. Round the margin of the enclosed area, which covers 28½ acres and was originally entered at three points, can be seen the remains of the largest megalithic circle in Europe, over 1,100 feet in diameter. The best idea of its original appearance may be had from the south-western sector, where many of the fallen stones have been raised. Within this circle the remains of two others, lesser in diameter but with larger stones, can be seen, to which must be added a third, set on the same axis, the site of which was discovered during the excavation of the northern entrance. This row of three circles evidently antedates the great bank and ditch, which, together with the Kennet Avenue belong to a later stage in the history of the site. The Avenue, which used to link the southern entrance of the great encirclement with the Sanctuary[1] more than a mile and a half distant on Overton Hill, was more complete in Stukeley's time. To-day, thanks to careful re-erection of some of the fallen stones, the final half mile of the sinuous approach has regained something of its former appearance.

The megaliths forming the avenue and various circles at Avebury were selected for their size and shape from vast numbers of sarsen stones which once covered stretches of the Wiltshire Downs. Small surviving tracts of the Grey Wethers, so called from their supposed resemblance by moonlight to a flock of

---

[1] To-day the Sanctuary is owned directly by the nation. In its earlier version the site comprised four concentric settings of timber uprights, but at the time of its attachment to Avebury these had been replaced by two rings of sarsen uprights. Concrete stumps have been placed to mark the former positions of timber and stone uprights, which latter were in course of removal when Stukeley visited the Sanctuary and made his sketch in 1723.

sheep, are preserved by the Trust at West Overton, Wiltshire, in Lockeridge and Piggle Denes, the latter adjoining the Bath road, about half-way between Marlborough and Avebury. In John Aubrey's day, so he tells us, the country-side round Marlborough looked "as if it had been the scene where the giants had fought with huge stones against the Gods". From these extensive fields of sarsen stones the Avebury megaliths were selected and dragged on some kind of slide to the scene of their erection, a labour which, taken in conjunction with the stupendous task of constructing the great amphitheatre enclosing the circles, presupposes some over-riding purpose on the part of the builders. At Avebury we are, indeed, in the presence of a temple, the grandest of its kind surviving from prehistoric Europe.

As was often the case with fanes of a later age, the temples founded in pre-historic times retained their sanctity long after the generation that built them had passed away. Not only were their structures modified over lengthy periods, but for generations they formed centres around which the dead were laid to rest. This is nowhere better seen than in the area surrounding Stonehenge, 1,442 acres of which are owned by the National Trust. Included in Trust property are about half the length of the Avenue, possibly a processional way, formed by parallel banks and ditches, which links Stonehenge to the Avon valley, and the greater part of the Cursus, a feature of unexplained use which may conceivably have been the scene of races held on festal occasions. But the most conspicuous features of the area are the numerous barrows, which include, in addition to the pre-existing long barrows, an accretion of some 300 round ones. In the mass these date from the early and middle stages of the Bronze Age, of which they are almost the sole reminder among the field monuments of Southern Britain. Barrows are scattered widely over the Stone-henge property, but certain groups deserve special mention, including the row of particularly fine bowl and bell barrows south of the Cursus and north-west of Stonehenge and the famous Winterbourne Stoke group on the south-western boundary. Between one and two hundred yards outside the southern boundary is the finest of all the Stonehenge series, the famous Normanton group, comprising nine bowl-, five disc-, two bell-, one twin bell- and two saucer-shaped round barrows, in addition to one long barrow. The Winter-bourne Stoke and Normanton groups, opened by William Cunnington and Sir Richard Colt Hoare in the first decade of the nineteenth century, proved to be the richest in Southern Britain. The bronzes, gold plating, amber and faience beads testify at once to the vigour of our British Bronze Age and to the wide-flung trade on which it was founded.

The equilibrium established after the Beaker invaders had been absorbed by the earlier inhabitants, was frequently disturbed during the first millenium B.C. under the impact of economic revolution and of movements of peoples. Owing to her remoteness from the main centres of unrest in Central Europe, Britain was at first affected during the Late Bronze Age mainly by industrial changes; prior to the middle of the eighth century B.C. immigration was con-fined to a few small groups who reached our south-eastern coasts, but failed to make any powerful impression farther inland. Only later did immigrants arrive in sufficient numbers to bring about significant cultural changes, introducing plough agriculture, new modes of burial and new kinds of pottery. Among the sites settled by immigrants at this time is Highdown Hill, five miles north-west of Worthing, Sussex, where their huts have been found under the rampart of the Iron Age hill-fort, which is the most prominent feature of this National Trust property. It may be noted that previous excavations disclosed an early Anglo-Saxon cemetery within the camp. This only serves to illustrate what a wide range of past activity some of our downland hilltops conceal.

Not until about 500 B.C. did migrant folk extensively equipped with iron begin to reach our shores. The Iron Age immigrations are far too complex for detailed treatment here and it must suffice to distinguish three of the more prominent episodes, of each of which the National Trust owns tangible memorials in the form of archaeological sites. The earliest and ethnically most important wave of immigration came from the European seaboard between the Rhine and Northern France. The culture of these early groups was a devolved version of that first recognized at Hallstatt in Austria, in which elements of the later culture named after the French site of La Tène were already infused. The National Trust can show in Figsbury, conspicuously sited on a promontory of the Wiltshire Downs in the parish of Winterbourne Dauntsey, a fine monument dating from an early stage of the first age of iron. Roughly circular in plan and having two entrances of the simplest character, Figsbury encloses a space of approximately 15 acres. When the rampart was sectioned, traces of three distinct structural phases could be seen, between each of which there had been time for turf to form; in other words, some while after the original construction, the rampart was strengthened on two separate occasions. The bulk of the material needed for the rampart was doubtless won from the great outer ditch, which with its V-shaped profile must have been a formidable element in the defences. Some, however, was obtained from a quarry-ditch opened within the enclosed area in such a position as to make the turf and chalk available in the handiest position for building into the rampart. To this day one can see, within the rampart with its outer defensive ditch, a second ditch, slighter and more irregularly cut. Although the interior of the enclosed area was extensively trenched, few signs of occupation were found. It seems evident that Figsbury served as a refuge for peasants dwelling in villages on the lower slopes of the Downs, like the well-known one at All Cannings Cross, with the pottery from which the few sherds from the hill-fort closely compare.

The next major episode in the British Early Iron Age was the arrival, in the middle of the third century B.C., of bands of warriors from the Marne district of Northern France. The warriors arrived in all the panoply of a developed La Tène culture, but since, as it would appear, they brought few women with them their coming was not sufficient to break the continuity of native tradition. The magnificent hill-fort at Cissbury is a product of this phase, built, we may suppose, by the natives, whether in self-defence or at the behest of the newly-established conquerors. To-day it is hard to visualize the defences as they once were, with a sharp, cleanly cut ditch and with the timber-revetted rampart set a few feet back from the lip. Formidable to attack, they must have been no less formidable to construct. The builders had first to quarry some 35,000 cubic yards of chalk and fell and prepare between 8 and 12,000 tree-trunk posts, before combining them to achieve an effective and stable result. It should also be remembered that Cissbury is only one of a number of such works on the chalk downs, products of the same wave of defensive preparation. The social cohesion and discipline implied in the erection of the hill-forts is not their least interesting aspect.

To complete the amalgam of prehistoric Britain came the Belgae, a people of mixed Celtic and Teutonic stock, who reached Kent probably by 75 B.C. and spread rapidly northwards into Hertfordshire, Cambridgeshire and Essex. One of the most important of their early settlements was that commanding a ford of the River Lea at Wheathampstead, a site now protected by the National Trust. The western side of what appears to be an enclosure of between 90 and 100 acres is formed by the very impressive Devil's Dyke, 130 feet from lip to lip and once as much as 40 feet in vertical depth. The early date of this site in the Belgic colonization is shown by the absence of imported pottery of Italic or South Gaulish type and of Belgic imitations, and it has been suggested that Wheathampstead may be none other than the *oppidum* of Cassivelaunus on which Caesar marched in 54 B.C. In due course the site lost its importance, which was transferred to the Belgic precursor of Verulamium, five or six miles to the south-west, close by a ford of the River Ver. From about the middle of the first century B.C. the Belgae began to spread westwards into Wessex. When ultimately they reached the Cotswold country, they threw up the system of dykes and embankments visible to-day on Minchinhampton and Rodborough Commons, possibly at the time of the Claudian Conquest.

The National Trust possesses no outstanding monuments dating from the initial wave of the Roman conquest, but it may be recalled that the area south-west of the Trent-Severn line, formally delimited not later than A.D. 47 by the Fosse Way and finally consolidated by the crushing of Boudicca's revolt in A.D. 61, was henceforth to constitute the core of the civilian zone of the province. The permanently military zone, a zone which formed part of the outer crust, as it were, of the Empire as a whole, was acquired in later phases of the conquest. Roman rule was extended progressively over the rest of England, over Wales and over much of Scotland under successive governors appointed by Vespasian. Between A.D. 71-74 Petillius Cerialis overwhelmed the Brigantes, occupied most of their territory and established a legionary fortress at York. His successor, Julius Frontinus, was responsible for conquering the Silures, setting up a second legionary fortress at Caerleon in South Wales and pressing forward into the central and northern parts of that country. The task of conquest was completed by Agricola. He began by incorporating North Wales and Anglesey; next he completed the subjugation of Brigantia, setting up the third legionary fortress at Chester; and lastly he invaded Scotland, first reducing the Lowlands as far as the Forth and Clyde, then in A.D. 83 destroying the assembled armies of the Highlands at the legendary "Mons Graupius". Only Ireland remained unconquered, when in the following year the governor was recalled to Rome.

With this second wave of conquest the Trust possesses links in two of Agricola's forts, associated respectively with his Welsh and Brigantian campaigns, namely Segontium (Caernarvon) and Ribchester. Archaeological excavation has revealed in the structural evolution of these forts, and more particularly in the case of Segontium, the main vicissitudes in the military history of the province. These auxiliary forts, built in the first instance of earth and timber, were reconstructed in stone early in the second century. At Segontium the rampart was cut back, faced with stone and provided with gates and turrets, and the timber buildings within were replaced by stone. The reconstruction at Segontium may have been hastened by fire, which partially destroyed the wooden buildings, but the process of substituting permanent for temporary materials was in the normal line of development at this time and is also met with at Ribchester. As commonly occurs at military sites, Segontium knew many abrupt ups and downs in its history. The first decline came towards the end of the second century A.D. and was doubtless a result of concentration by the legions on the building of Hadrian's Wall.

For the generation following Agricola's recall, history has little to tell of the Roman province. The attention of the rulers of the Empire was diverted to other regions and the former governor of Britain died a disappointed man. It is likely that the northern conquests were maintained until the close of the first century, but thereafter they were allowed to slip away. The policy of withdrawal implied at some stage the delimitation of a northern frontier. The first line selected was that of the Stanegate, the road running from Carlisle to the North Tyne a few miles south of the western part of the frontier as it was later defined. Systematic fortification of the Stanegate, undertaken in the time of Trajan, was, however, but a first step. Definitive action was delayed until the Emperor Hadrian in person visited the province and planned the great wall that bears his name.

Since its course was first surveyed in 1599 by Camden, Hadrian's Wall has come to be regarded as a national monument by many English people and it is good to know that the National Trust now owns some 3½ miles of its length, including in Housesteads one of its most famous forts. The Wall combines the Roman idea of a *limes*, essentially a frontier road equipped with forts and signal towers, with the Germanic conception of a continuous barrier. It comprises a powerful wall, fronted by a ditch thirty feet across, with a military road to the rear, extending from Bowness-on-Solway to Wallsend-on-Tyne, an overall distance of more than seventy miles. Disposed along its length are sixteen forts, while built into it at intervals of a Roman mile are fortlets, between each of which are two turrets or signalling stations. Close behind the Wall and its military road is the broad, deep, flat-bottomed ditch, having banks some 20 feet from either lip and known to antiquaries as the Vallum. The relationship of Wall and Vallum was for long a bone of contention, but to-day they are recognized as contemporary works. The function of the Vallum was to define the defensive zone on its inner or southern side and so ease the task of controlling both the movement of men and the flow of trade across the frontier.

25 The "Cerne Giant", Dorset

26 Stones of the Coldrum Barrow, Kent

28 Hadrian's Wall near Housesteads, Northumberland

29, 30   Mosaic Pavements of the Roman Villa at Chedworth, in the Cotswolds

The wall itself is of composite construction. As originally planned, only the eastern portion from the first starting point at Newcastle as far west as Irthing was to be of stone build; the remaining 30 miles or so were to be of turf or clay, whichever was nearest to hand. The project was modified as work proceeded. The wall was extended eastwards to cover the last reach of the tidal Tyne; its thickness was reduced from ten to eight feet; and it was decided to carry the stone build along its whole length, replacing the earlier western portions of turf and clay by the more durable material. Finally, it must be remembered that what we see are essentially the ruins, not of the original, but of the wall as it was reconstructed by the Emperor Severus after the disaster of 197 A.D.

The building of the wall was an immense achievement, a very "monument to Roman purposiveness", as he will testify who follows its majestic course on the ground. The ditch involved the quarrying of nearly two million cubic yards of rock, some of it of extreme hardness, and the wall itself incorporated rather more than this volume of material. For the western part of the wall's course its substance had all to be transported. Even where the stone was available, the facing stones had to be dressed and the mortar prepared. In addition the numerous forts, fortlets and turrets had all to be constructed, as well as the military road and numerous bridges. Further, the Vallum has been estimated to have consumed "a million man-days of labour in mere earth-work". The work was undertaken in the main by the legions, but at least one section was built by men of the fleet. During the Severan rebuilding it may be noted that four British tribes have been recorded as having worked as independent units.

If the Wall was mainly built by legionaries, it was garrisoned by auxiliary troops. Each of the forts held an auxiliary regiment, sheltering in the aggregate an establishment of about 10,000 men. Another 4,000 may have been held by the northern outposts and by the forts on the Cumberland coast. If the patrolling garrison, based on the fortlets and turrets, accounted for another 5,000, this would give a total of some 19,000 auxiliaries. It has been estimated that, if we allow for troops quartered within two or three days' march, some fifty out of the sixty-eight auxiliary regiments in the province were used to support the northern frontier. To the rear stood the legions at York and Chester, while the third at Caerleon stood guard behind the western frontier.

The Wall was designed as a measure of control and was skilfully placed so as to command an extensive sweep of country. From it the enemy could be observed from a distance and behind it the requisite forces could be marshalled at the crucial point. In case of need the auxiliaries would sally out through the gates and break up any hostile formation before the Wall. Thus was the frontier guarded with the minimum of force. Only twice did the northern barbarians pass the line of the Wall prior to its final abandonment. On the first occasion in A.D. 197 this was due, not to any deficiencies in the frontier works, but to the withdrawal of troops from the province in support of the imperial pretensions of the Governor Albinus. The Caledonian tribes systematically wrecked the Wall and its forts and carried destruction as far south as the legionary fortresses of York and Chester. When Severus, winner of the struggle for the Empire, decided that the frontier should be restored, he did not find it necessary to devise a new system, but only to rebuild on the old and well-tried lines. In the first decade of the third century Rome was still sure of herself. As another item in the programme of reconstruction the fort of Segontium was rebuilt with substantially enlarged administrative quarters.

There is a melancholy in the twilight of Roman military power in Britain. When Segontium was next reconstructed, the work was carried out not to over-awe the native population, but to protect it from western sea-rovers. In A.D. 367-9 the assaults of the barbarians reached a climax: Scots from Ireland fell upon the western coasts, Saxons from Germany descended on the eastern seaboard and Picts assailed the northern frontier of the distracted province, broke the Wall and wasted Brigantia. When, following the usurpation of Maximus in A.D. 383, the Picts broke the Wall a second time, this proved a final blow. The Wall was never again restored.

For more than quarter of a millenium Hadrian's Wall had formed a northern bulwark of the Roman world; let us now turn to Housesteads,[1] the most completely explored of the forts which lodged its garrisons. When Dr. Stukeley and Roger Gale visited the site in 1725 they "were surprised with the august scene of Romano-British antiquities, in the most neglected condition". Rather more than a hundred years later the walls and the entrances were laid bare and during the last decade of the nineteenth century the interior was systematically excavated. In plan the fort is of normal type, a parallelogram with rounded corners, having a double portal in each wall. The rampart, which encloses nearly 5 acres, consists of an earth bank with stone facing, up to a dozen courses of which are still in place. Roman wheel-ruts worn 8 inches in the stone threshold can be seen at the east gateway, and the visitor who cares to measure will find that the gauge (4 ft. 8½ ins.) is the same as that standard on English railways. West of the north gate a catapult emplacement is still visible and stone shot weighing from 1 to 1½ cwt. were found during the excavations. At the south gate the central pier still shows signs of the dislo-cation thought to have been caused at the time of the disaster near the end of the second century. Within the fort most of the space was occupied by barrack buildings, but the headquarters and the house of the commandant are promin-ent. Other features are the granaries for supplying the garrison and at the south-east corner the fresh-water acqueduct and the latrines. Outside, to the west, the grass-grown foundations of the suburbs can still be seen and cultiva-tion terraces line the high ground. On Chapel Hill, a rocky ridge beyond the suburban settlement, there is a semi-subterranean temple dedicated to Mithras, whose cult, introduced to Europe from Persia about the time of Julius Caesar, was popular among frontier troops. The cemetery was sited south and east of the fort on low ground.

In the civilian part of the province Romanized life centred on the towns and villas. To the Roman conquerors, indeed, the city was in itself the essence of civilization, and the foundation of cities a necessary step in the civilizing of a

[1] Owned by the Trust and the 316-acre farm in which it stands is protected by covenants. The museum was built by the Trust.

new province. Up to the present the National Trust owns no characteristic city site, but it is important to remember that the planning of cities on the classical model was a feature of Flavian Britain. Well-paved streets were laid out on the familiar chess-board plan and the usual public buildings—markets, halls of justice, temples, public baths and amphitheatres—were erected on a generous scale. Private buildings in the form of dwelling houses and shops rarely attained the standard set by the public edifices. To give some idea of scale, the 100 acres enclosed by the city walls of Silchester were but sparsely settled and the population was probably well below the common estimate of 2,000. As the largest city in the province London had an area of 330 acres and a population of perhaps 15,000. At no time did city life flourish as it did in Gaul, where the tradition of town dwelling had more vigorous roots in the native culture. When, about the middle of the third century, city life throughout the Empire entered on a period of decline, the focus of Romanized life in the province of Britain shifted to the villas. Before turning to the rural life of the province, we may pause a moment at one of the smaller properties of the Trust, an acre of ground at Wall in Staffordshire, where buildings of the ancient *Letocetum* have been excavated. Exceptionally well preserved are the baths, where weary travellers, as well as its inhabitants, may have found refreshment. For *Letocetum* was a small township grown up around a posting station on Watling Street, one of the great strategic highways, radiating from London, which knit together the civilian and military zones of the province.

In the countryside two separate economic systems co-existed, one remaining predominantly native in character, the other a focus of Romanization. Of the native peasantry, who probably maintained in most essentials the culture of their prehistoric forebears, it is unnecessary to say much here. Yet it is important to remember that these people were a substantial, indeed a numerically predominant element in the population of the province. It was the Romano-British peasants who cultivated so many of the Celtic fields still visible on our upland soils, especially on the chalk of Southern England. Until more of their settlements have been investigated by modern methods, it will not be possible to say how far Roman civilization modified the prehistoric folk-culture of the broad masses of the rural population.

The villas have long been recognized as the country homes of the Romanized gentry, but it is only comparatively lately that their importance as centres of agricultural estates has been appreciated. It is eloquent of the two-fold division of the province that of the 500 odd villas at present known some 90 per cent lie south-east of the Trent-Severn line. Already in the latter half of the first century villa life had taken root in Kent, parts of Hampshire and the Isle of Wight, and by the end of the century it had spread to Somerset and the Thames Valley. During the years that followed the villas prospered exceedingly. Gaining from the eclipse of the towns, they entered on their golden age in the fourth century.

Of the three classes into which the country houses may be divided the humblest was basilican in plan, consisting of an oblong barn-like structure divided into nave and aisles by two internal rows of posts. The most numerous class was the corridor villa, in which a row of rooms, up to twenty in number, was fronted or in some cases surrounded by a corridor or veranda. The finest villas were those built round one or more courtyards, commonly with from thirty to forty rooms. Of this last class the Trust possesses an excellent example at Chedworth, near Cirencester. Discovered in 1864, when tesserae were noticed in soil thrown up in digging out a ferret in Lord Eldon's park, the villa was extensively excavated two years later. To-day most of the plan can be made out and the finds brought to light during the excavations may be studied in the museum on the site. Among the many details which remind us of the pervasive influence of Roman civilization may be noted the mosaic pavements in what was probably the dining-room, one of them illustrating a dance symbolic of the seasons, the well-preserved baths, the worn steps of which testify to common use, and the hypocaust, remains of the central heating system. But it would be wrong to dwell on a note of luxury or ease. The villas were assuredly centres of Roman manners, but they were also the administrative hubs of substantial estates. The farmyard or compound with its barns, threshing-floor and well were essential adjuncts of the villa itself, which housed not only the owner and his family, but also all the workers needed on the estate. The economics of the villa, as later of the manor, were basically those of sub-sistence. Not only food production, but many accessory occupations, such as carpentry and smithing, were based on the villa. The iron pigs, weighing from 256 to 484 pounds, found in an enclosure at the north-west corner of the Chedworth Villa, suggest that many at least of the iron objects now preserved in the museum were made on the estate. Occasionally indications are found of industries on a more than domestic scale. The tanks and furnaces on the north side of the inner courtyard at Chedworth show that fulling was carried out in a large way, an activity for which the plentiful supply of water and the nearby bed of fuller's earth made the site peculiarly well fitted.

The pagan altars and the slabs at Chedworth, inscribed by masons with the Christian Chi-Rho symbol, remind us of the part played by religion in Roman Britain. Great diversity is apparent. The official cult, headed by Juppiter Optimus Maximus and the members of the Roman pantheon, co-existed on terms of amity with numerous local cults of the old Celtic deities. In addition, there were Celtic deities from the continent, eastern cults such as Mithraism, met with on the Wall, and not least Christianity. Introduced in underground fashion at least as early as the second century, Christianity gathered momentum in the third century and, surviving persecution under Diocletian, emerged into the light of day during the fourth century. Making its appeal mainly to the poor, the new religion left only the scantiest traces in Roman Britain and the furtive symbols scratched on the stone slabs of Chedworth are in this sense deeply typical. The official cult itself offered a wide range of choice in the attention paid to the lesser gods. Mercury and Mars were the most popular in the province, but Neptune, Sylvanus and Hercules each had a goodly following. The cult of Hercules received a powerful impetus when in A.D. 191 the Emperor Commodus declared himself an incarnation of the god. This is of special interest to us, because in the Giant of Cerne the National Trust possesses an outstanding memorial of his cult. The figure of the Giant, cut in the turf of the Dorset Downs above the village of Cerne Abbas, stands 180 feet in height, to which the knotty club brandished in the right hand adds another 35 feet. The suggestion of Bronze Age antiquity is quite baseless. In fact, the Giant differs markedly in style from the only hill-figure of proved prehistoric date, the White Horse of Uffington, the convention of which is clearly in the manner of the late Celtic school, evinced in the coinage and repoussé work of Belgic Britain. The figure of Hercules is rendered, on the contrary, with all the clumsy naturalism of Romano-British art. We may take leave of the Giant as a symbol of Rome cut in the turf of a British down.

Acknowledgement

The author acknowledges his indebtedness to Sir Cyril Fox, Archaeological Adviser to the National Trust, who read this chapter in typescript and offered helpful criticism.

Inside of Bodiam Castle Gate, Sussex   June 1st 1784

31 Bodiam Castle, Sussex: Vaulted Vestibule in the Entrance Tower.
From a water colour by S. H. Grimm (1784)

IV

MEDIEVAL BUILDINGS

By JOHN H. HARVEY

LIFE flows on, and cannot be divided into neat sections of equal length, yet for historical purposes it is convenient to choose arbitrary periods which conform to some basic plan of existence. In Europe such a period is formed by what we call the Middle Ages, set between the Classic World of Greece and Rome, and the modern days in which we live.

Not the whole of the time which elapsed between the breakdown of Rome and the Renaissance of Roman learning can fairly be included in the Middle Ages, for the five centuries following the withdrawal of the Legions were in themselves an age of darkness in which two great forces, the open-air vitality of the northern folk, and the classic culture of the Mediterranean under a Christian guise, struggled for supremacy and ultimately achieved equilibrium.

Only after the Danish invasions of the ninth century and the new stabilisation of national life under King Alfred does English history begin: before Alfred there was no English nation, and few written records remain. What we know of the pre-Roman, Roman, and Saxon eras we owe to the archaeologist rather than to the historian, while for the past millenium we depend in the first place upon the written word. The end of the period must be sought in the reign of Henry VIII, to whom is due the total nature of the change which, for better or for worse, altered the complexion of English life between 1500 and 1550.

It is singular that the aptest description of the contrast between the two warring forces of the Dark Age should have been spoken in feudal China a thousand years earlier. Confucius defined the energy of southern regions as showing forbearance and gentleness, while to lie under arms and meet death without regret was the study of the forceful men of the north. To some degree the English compromise approached his ideal, the man firm in energy who stands erect in the middle, cultivating a friendly harmony without being weak.[1]

Many centuries were to pass before this solution was reached, and in them may be observed a fascinating interplay between the two forces, which found their outward symbols in the castle and the convent. Unlike the fortresses of the Roman Empire, which were wholly military, the English castle, with few exceptions, was first of all a residence, wherein men might live in comparative safety, in spite of the burden of defence.

The monastic ideal, on the other hand, sought peace in withdrawal from the affairs of the world behind a spiritual barrier. As the centuries passed by, castle and cloister grew to resemble each other: while the growth of royal justice rendered private fortification less and less necessary, greater luxury became possible in the purely domestic sections of the fortress: at the same time

[1] *The Doctrine of the Mean*, Chapter X.

men were becoming less amenable to the spiritual terrors of excommunication and increasingly envious of the hoarded riches of ecclesiastical landlords—in consequence the larger monasteries took upon them the likeness of castles, provided with frowning gatehouses and high ramparts.

Internally, the men of religion in most cases found less and less to attract them in a spiritual life, and turned their abbeys into private mansions, provided with comfortable rooms and panelled chambers instead of the bleak dormitory and draughty frater. The monks, and their later rivals the friars, steadily lost touch with the religious needs of their flock, and wealthy individuals sought rest for their souls by founding colleges of secular priests, whose common life was limited to the services of their church, while they were otherwise free to come and go in the outer world.

The less wealthy joined gilds and fraternities, rather like modern friendly societies in their aims, but with the added benefit of having a gild chapel where chaplains would sing masses perpetually for the souls of deceased members. Great numbers of smaller chantries were founded by individuals and families, who also joined in the life of their parish church, which served not only as a place of worship, but often as a town-hall, a warehouse, and even as a convenient place for dances and feasts.

The parish churches and parochial chapels, though their uses are not now so varied, are still under the care of the national Church, while civic buildings and domestic houses are generally used for their original purposes, where they have survived at all. For the castle and the convent, however, there is no normal place in modern life, and their remains would soon vanish if steps were not taken to preserve them. It is a healthy symptom in our national life that the English are reluctant to push matters to their logical conclusion or to act under regimentation in accordance with official plans. Thus it comes about that the preservation of national monuments has been mainly due to private enterprise; first the protective and advisory work of the Society for the Preservation of Ancient Buildings; secondly, permanent preservation through ownership by the National Trust. Only at a later date came a national scheme of protection and repair in the Ancient Monuments Act of 1913.

In view of the extensive and specialized structural works which are often required, the majority of ruins now protected are under the guardianship of the Ministry of Works, who have produced an admirable series of regional guides to the buildings under their control, prepared by the Right Honourable W. Ormsby Gore, now Lord Harlech, when First Commissioner of Works. These guides have introduced the subject to a wide public, and provide an admirable background, beside giving details of all the buildings actually in the ownership or guardianship of the Ministry. The smaller number of remains owned by the National Trust are of equal interest, though possibly less spectacular than those in official hands, and the attempt will here be made to show something of their importance as integral parts of the national heritage.

The lifetime of King Alfred saw a whole culture wiped out and a new beginning made; together with the barbarous but brilliant early Saxon Courts, the last vestiges of British Christianity and of Augustine's monasticism were

33 The Tower on Glastonbury Tor, Somerset

32 Westbury College, Bristol

34　Hayles Abbey, Gloucestershire: the ruined Chapter-house and Cloister

35　Lacock Abbey, Wiltshire: the Cloisters

swept away, even the ancient sanctuary of Glastonbury being ravaged. Anyone who has climbed Glastonbury Tor in winter when the floods are out, will realize what a pertinacious fury it was that could carry the Northmen to the Isle of Avalon.

Through the tenth century Alfred's work of reconstruction was carried on, at first by laymen and secular clerics, but in the second half of the century Benedictine monasticism was reintroduced by Oswald, Bishop of Worcester in 961, and later Archbishop of York. Oswald had been educated at the great Benedictine house of Fleury on the Loire, the centre of the revival, and no sooner was he installed at Worcester than he founded a house of the order at Westbury-on-Trym, close to Bristol, on lands which had been granted to the see in 804. After a life of only fifteen years the community was transferred to Ramsey in Huntingdonshire in 974, and of Westbury nothing more is heard for a century. By the irony of fate, its later history exactly reversed its original position: in the tenth century it had been the spearpoint of that great monastic movement which was to give the Benedictine order a measure of control over English church life for nearly six centuries; in the end it was to be used as a lever to dislodge that same monastic power. At the end of the thirteenth century Bishop Giffard attempted to become Bishop of Worcester and Westbury, in order to escape from the power of the Benedictines at Worcester, as the bishops of Lichfield had escaped from Coventry and those of Wells from Bath, but he was unsuccessful. By the middle of the fifteenth century the bishop's position was still more unbearable, and Bishop John Carpenter refounded Westbury as a College, beginning to rebuild the church and to erect the College buildings, part of which remain, in 1447. He adopted the style of Bishop of Worcester and Westbury, and in the teeth of monastic opposition endowed almshouses out of the revenues of the see and in 1463 appropriated to the College the Church of Clifton on condition that the Dean and Chapter should find a master to teach grammar (i.e. Latin) without charge to any persons whomsoever who came to him. King Edward IV was a generous benefactor, and from 1469 to 1474 the Dean was William Caninges, the rich merchant who had been five times Mayor of Bristol and finally took holy orders.

All this lay hidden in the distant future when Benedictine rule was in its first strength in the tenth and eleventh centuries. When Edward the Confessor regained the throne from the Danish dynasty he hastened to bring over Norman advisers, many of whom were Benedictines, for whose benefit the King undertook his great rebuilding of Westminster Abbey, begun in 1050. Among the Norman laymen Robert FitzWimarc was prominent; it was to Robert's home at Clavering in Essex that the Norman favourites fled on hearing of Earl Godwin's return from banishment in 1052.

In 1066 Robert attempted to dissuade William from invading England, but supported him after Hastings, and received new grants of land; both Robert and his son Suen after him were Sheriffs of Essex and Hertfordshire. After Robert's death, Suen left Clavering and built himself a castle at Rayleigh; in 1086 the compilers of Domesday made special mention that in one of his four manors "Suen has made his castle". Rayleigh Mount was thus one of the first

Norman castles to be built, probably at the Conqueror's instructions, to keep down the Saxon population in the Home Counties. It consisted of a high motte or mound, which still exists, with an outer and an inner bailey surrounded by mounds and palisades; the inner bailey was later defended by a stone wall, but only its fragmentary foundations have survived.

Suen's son Robert adhered to the party of Matilda, against Stephen; thus his son, Henry of Essex, was in great favour with Henry II, who made him standard-bearer, but it was this honourable office which led to his downfall. In 1157 King Henry undertook an expedition against the Welsh, but was ambushed, and in the sudden emergency Henry of Essex flung down the standard and joined in the headlong rout. He was challenged as a traitor by Robert de Montfort and finally the case came to combat in 1163; Henry was overcome and fell, and the monks of Reading were given permission to bury him. After reaching the Abbey he was found to be alive, recovered, and joined the community, but his lands, including Rayleigh, were forfeit to the King. For some time the Castle was kept in repair, and King John visited it in 1214, but in the following year the Honor was granted to Hubert de Burgh, no mention of the castle being made. De Burgh built a new castle at Hadleigh near the coast, and as early as 1277 the site of Rayleigh had become grazing ground. The remains of masonry were thoroughly cleared away by the local inhabitants, who in 1394 obtained permission from Richard II to take and carry off the stones of the "foundation of a certain old castle which used to be there" to repair a chapel and build a belfry in the town.

Of even greater importance than Rayleigh, and likewise built soon after the Conquest, was Duffield Castle. It was the work of Henry de Ferrers, a companion of the Conqueror; Henry's son Robert distinguished himself at the battle of Northallerton in 1138 and was created Earl of Derby. The immense stone keep whose foundations remain was probably built during the twelfth century, but belonged to an earlier stage in the development of the donjon than the high tower-keeps devised by Master Maurice, Henry II's military expert, who built Newcastle in 1171-77, and Dover keep ten years later.

Duffield's foundations show that it was 99 feet long by 93 feet wide; it thus exceeded in size all the Norman keeps except Colchester, the Tower of London, and Dover; and except for Dover had the thickest walls. The Ferrers earldom persisted until Robert, sixth in descent from Henry, joined de Montfort against Henry III. In 1265 he threw himself upon the King's mercy, but after the most solemn undertakings began a new revolt and was defeated at Chesterfield on the 15th of May, 1266, and captured. He was discovered, it is said owing to information given by a girl whose lover he had compelled to fight among the rebels, hiding between sacks of wool stored in Chesterfield Church. The Ferrers lands were bestowed on Prince Edmund immediately, but the King took the precaution of having Duffield Castle razed to the ground. Nothing was left but burnt debris and some few carved stones flung down the well, where they crushed the bucket at the bottom, to be found and restored, an almost unique specimen, when the site was excavated in 1886. Though the castle had gone, its site was remembered, for in 1588, the year of the Armada,

36   Lindisfarne Castle, Holy Island, Northumberland

37   Cilgerran Castle, Pembrokeshire: from the painting by
Richard Wilson in the National Museum of Wales

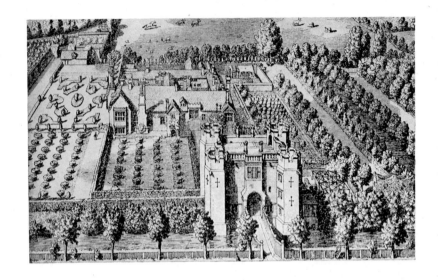

38, 39   Boarstall Tower, Buckinghamshire, in an engraving of 1695, and to-day

a doggerel versifier of Duffield, Anthony Bradshawe, produced a series of quatrains more interesting for their topographical than their poetic qualities; one tells us:

> At Duffield Placehead, placed was a statlye Castly and Cortyard
> Whereof the seyte yet beareth name now called Castly Orchard.
> The Duke there had great royalties of forest p'ks of warren
> And wards and pleines of waters store, of grounds not very barren.

Contrasting with these Norman fortresses, let us consider the priory of Austin Canons founded at Merton in Surrey in 1115. Temporary buildings of timber were first erected, then two years later new buildings were set up on another site, and in 1130 the foundations of the stone church were laid. Probably the precinct wall was among the first works undertaken on the new site in 1117. Hardly anything else remains above ground, though the plan of the church was recovered by excavation in 1925. The history of the Priory was almost the history of England during the period of its existence, for it was specially favoured by royalty, forming as it did a pleasant place to stay at, a short journey from the capital. There was even a royal suite of apartments, for whose repair in 1258 Henry III sent Master John of Gloucester, his chief mason. Thomas Becket began his schooling at Merton; the Statutes of Merton were promulgated there in 1236; Henry III granted oak timber for the rebuilding of the church after the tower had been blown down in a great storm in the winter of 1222, and later ordered a cross to be set up outside the gate in memory of William Earl of Warenne and Surrey, who died in 1240.

Hubert de Burgh in 1232 fled to Merton for sanctuary from the angry citizens of London, and William of Wykeham took refuge there in 1376 when banished from the court. The right of sanctuary was one of the greatest contributions made by the Church in mitigation of a lawless age, and though it was a privilege greatly abused in later days, there can be no doubt that it was urgently needed in the early Middle Ages, and at all the greater churches there were elaborate regulations for the due observance of the place of refuge. At Ripon an area extending roughly for a mile in each direction from the great Church of St. Wilfrid was marked out by eight crosses. Of these crosses, that at Sharow alone exists, and now comprises only the stump of a square shaft built into a base of roughly squared stones. Unfortunately no records of the Ripon sanctuary exist, but those of Durham and Beverley contain a few instances of Ripon men who sought sanctuary elsewhere, and give a vivid picture of the fugitive's arrival, whereupon the bells were rung, witnesses were summoned, and the petitioner straightway made full confession of the facts which were taken down and witnessed, often by the craftsmen who would be at work in the church at the time. On two occasions at Durham, in 1515 and 1519, the Master Mason Christopher Scoyne was a witness; he was also in charge of the rebuilding of Ripon nave and had recently built the fine spire of Louth in Lincolnshire.

Perhaps connected with Merton Priory was the ancient Chapel at West Humble, a hamlet of Mickleham in Surrey; the ruins stand close to Chapel

Farm, a Merton property, but separated from the farm buildings by a road. The manor of West Humble belonged to Reigate Priory, but since West Humble lies across the River Mole from Mickleham and was often cut off by floods in winter, it seems most probable that it was a chapel-of-ease for that tithing of Mickleham, west of the river. The ragged flint remains of the gable-ends and foundations of the south wall are all that is left, and suggest a date of 1200 or soon after.

Another interesting chapel is that at Buckingham, which retains a late twelfth-century South doorway; later it became the chapel of the earliest chantry in Buckinghamshire, founded by Matthew Stratton, Archdeacon of Buckinghamshire 1223-68. About 1475 it was largely rebuilt by John Ruding, Canon of Lincoln and Prebendary of Buckingham (for the enormous diocese of Lincoln stretched down to the Thames), and most of the existing building is his work. After the chantries were dissolved it long continued in use as the Latin School, doubtless maintaining the earlier teaching offered by the chantry priests.

Far off in the north lies the lonely hamlet of Keld, with a little chapel-of-ease built, or possibly rebuilt, at the very end of the Middle Ages; its simple form and square-headed east window of three uncusped lights suggest a date shortly before the Reformation. Similar windows are found in the top storey of Abbot Huby's tower at Fountains Abbey, built before 1526, probably to the design of that Master Christopher Scoyne whom we have already met. Scoyne and the northern masons were experimenting with a simple style, and for another example we may go to the parish church of Burnley, Lancashire, where two masons, Nicholas Craven and Thomas Sellers built the north and south aisles between 1533 and 1537—here too the windows are square-headed, with cuspless elliptical heads to the lights, in striking contrast to the richly-carved late Perpendicular churches of the South of England.

Before returning to the main thread of development, one minor monument should be mentioned, the Market Cross at Colston Bassett, Nottinghamshire. It is typical of a large class built to give a religious sanction to the transactions of everyday life. Pillars standing at cross-roads had similar significance in pre-Christian times, like the Roman wayside statues of Mercury against which the traveller threw a stone "for luck". The market cross of Christian times was of course presided over not by the god of merchants, but by the cross or the crucifix. At Colston Bassett, the original shaft and head have disappeared, and the base was rebuilt with an incongruous classic column for shaft, to commemorate the coronation of William IV in 1831. The cross stands on its old site, for it appeared in the same position on a map of 1604, and it was presumably here that a cross was erected by Ralph Bassett in 1257, when he had obtained from Henry III the grant of a weekly market and a yearly fair of three days, on the vigil, feast, and morrow of St. Faith, the sixth of October. The present base cannot be so early, but is an unusually fine moulded stone, perhaps a relic of rebuilding in the fifteenth century.

The great age of monastic foundations in England came soon after the Conquest, and these abbeys and priories were of course in the heavy, round-arched Romanesque style. Splendid examples of their churches remain at

Durham, at Peterborough, and in a mutilated condition at St. Bartholomew the Great, London. Grand as they are, these buildings reflect the semi-barbarous nature of the age which built them, and their style offered little scope for structural progress or aesthetic refinements. Such refinements were soon called for, for in 1099 the First Crusade captured Jerusalem and through the first half of the twelfth century a stream of returning Crusaders and merchants brought to the West a taste for the luxuries of their Saracen opponents, and a rudimentary knowledge of Eastern art. The pointed arch spread through Western Europe, and was seized upon by the master masons as the device of which they stood in most need. With the pointed arch as a basis for the new science of ribbed vaulting, a new style was swiftly developed, and soon after 1150 began to reach England. By the 1170's two schools of transitional architecture had reached us: one at Wells in Somerset, where the cathedral was entirely rebuilt, except for the west front, between 1175 and 1206; the other at Canterbury, where after a disastrous fire an architectural competition was held, won by the French master, William of Sens, who rebuilt the choir between 1174 and 1177, when he was crippled by a fall from the scaffolding. The work was carried on in an even more advanced Gothic style by his assistant, William the Englishman. The finest general views of Wells and Canterbury Cathedrals are obtained from the Tor Hill, south-east of Wells, and Golden Hill, Harbledown, a mile to the west of Canterbury.

The Crusades, partially responsible for Gothic architecture, also produced a singular blend of opposing forces in the Military Orders. Of these the Hospitallers originated as guardians of the hospital or hospice for pilgrims in Jerusalem. At first Benedictine monks, these guardians were formed into a new order in 1113, and soon afterwards imitated the Templars in taking on a military character. Introduced into England, their first priory was that at Clerkenwell, begun in 1144, and during the next half century their possessions rapidly increased, each group of lands being administered by a small number of knights under a commander. The commanderies were usually equivalent to a manor house, and a surviving example is St. John's Jerusalem, at Sutton-at-Hone in Kent. Robert de Basing had given his manor in Sutton to the Hospitallers in 1199, and soon afterwards a new house was built. Henry III stayed at the commandery, and in 1234 ordered five oaks to be given to the keeper there for the roofing of the chapel. This chapel, whose date is thus accurately fixed, is the principal existing portion of the mediaeval building, and has three beautiful lancet windows in the east wall, under a triple hood-moulding supported on delicate attached shafts. The King's goodwill may have provided not only materials, but also an architect, in the person of John of Waverley, a Cistercian lay-brother, who at this time was in charge of some of the King's building operations.

Brother John of Waverley was a trained mason, and had presumably been engaged on the building of Waverley Abbey in Surrey, where the work of the quire and transepts was ready for consecration in 1231. From 1237 to 1239 Brother John devised works in Westminster Palace, and in 1251 he was sent to Darnhall in Cheshire to build a new concrete retaining wall for the King's fish-pond, but in the intervening period his name disappears from the public records. Owing to a passing reference, we know that during part of the time he was building the Cistercian Abbey of Hayles in Gloucestershire.

Richard, Earl of Cornwall, brother of Henry III, was returning from Bordeaux in 1242 when he was almost cast away by tempest, and vowed that in the event of survival he would build an Abbey of Cistercian monks. After his return he obtained the manor and advowson of Hayles and within the five years 1246-51 the church and the greater part of the claustral buildings were carried to completion. The plan of Hayles closely follows that of Waverley, rather than that of Beaulieu, Hants, from which it was colonized, and the Hayles plan was followed at Netley, where the church was begun in 1251 under the patronage of Henry III. Both Hayles and Netley derived some of their inspiration from the French ideas brought to Westminster for the new Abbey church by the King's mason, Master Henry of Reyns, but the fragments of a great geometric window must belong to the second work at Hayles, begun after a fire in 1271. This second work consisted in the replacement of the square east end by a chevet of five polygonal chapels radiating from a central space in which stood the shrine of the Holy Blood, brought to Hayles by Edmund, son of Earl Richard in 1270. The chevet was directly copied from that at Westminster, and may have been designed by Master Robert of Beverley, the King's chief mason from 1261 to 1284; it was probably from this new work of Hayles that Tewkesbury Abbey copied its own chevet some forty years later.

For an unexpected picture of life at Hayles in 1417 we must go to the extra-ordinary "Book of Margery Kempe", whose methodistical ecstasies must have been a sore trial to almost all she met. In 1417 she went on pilgrimage to St. James of Compostella, but before being allowed to leave Bristol was haled before the Bishop of Worcester "who lay three miles beyond Bristol", at Westbury, where she reproved his fashionably-dressed esquires to their great annoyance, but was hospitably entertained by the Bishop until her ship was ready to sail. On her return "she abode not long [at Bristol], but went forth to the Blood of Hayles, and there she was shriven and had loud cries and boisterous weepings. Then the religious men had her in amongst them, and made her good cheer, save they swore many great oaths and horrible. And she rebuked them there-for, after the Gospel, and thereof had they great wonder. Nevertheless some were right well pleased, thanked be God for His goodness."

Rather earlier than Hayles was the Abbey of Lacock, Wiltshire, founded by Ela, wife of William Longsword, Earl of Salisbury, in 1232, and built within the next few years. The church has gone, but the claustral buildings remain, though altered into a large mansion. Of exceptional beauty is the original chapter house, and the three walks of the Perpendicular cloister are extremely fine. The rebuilding of the cloister began towards the end of the fourteenth century and was carried on through the fifteenth, to which period belongs the unusual vaulting, having instead of bosses, small polygonal panels at its main intersections. This peculiarity also occurs in the vault of the Beauchamp Chapel at Warwick, built 1441-52, and in the cloister vaults at Wells, built

40   Bodiam Castle, Sussex

41, 42 Tattershall Castle,
Lincolnshire, and one of
its great fireplaces

by John Turpyn, mason of Wells, about 1457. The designer of the Warwick vault is unknown, though Thomas Kerver of Warwick may perhaps have been responsible, for it is improbable that the royal craftsmen from London who were called in for the decoration and glazing, would have introduced this West of England peculiarity. At Hayles also are remains of a new cloister, begun about 1475 and still in progress within a few years of the Dissolution.

Though not properly conventual buildings, mention may here be made of Steventon Priory Cottages, Berkshire, which are said to represent the small alien priory founded as a result of Henry I's gift of Steventon to the priory of Notre Dame du Pré by Rouen, a cell of the Abbey of Bec. There never were monastic buildings, since the monks used the parish church for their offices, and the religious comprised only the prior and one companion. Conse-quently their dwelling was to all intents and purposes a normal house; at Steventon an inventory taken in 1324 tells us that there were then a chamber, hall, pantry and buttery, larder, kitchen, brewhouse and dairy. Evidently the two monks employed a number of lay servants, for the kitchen contained twenty plates, twenty dishes, and twenty saucers of wood, as well as the usual pots, pans and other culinary impedimenta. The wars between France and England led to the estates of these alien religious houses being taken into the King's hand again and again, and finally most of them were confiscated by Henry V in 1414. Many, foreseeing the end, had had the wisdom to realize on their possessions while they could, and Steventon was leased to Sir Hugh Calveley in 1361, again for forty years in 1378, and two years later he had custody of the property for life. From the mid-fourteenth century therefore, Steventon ceased to have even a shadow of corporate religious life, and the buildings became a mere farmhouse. If the Priory Cottages have been correctly identified, it is just possible that the hall is substantially that of 1324, for its roof had originally a massive tie-beam of early type, altered in the fifteenth century, into a hammer-beam truss after hammer beams had been made popular by Master Hugh Herland's wonderful roof of Westminster Hall, finished in 1400.

The confiscation of alien priories was the precedent for the piecemeal aboli-tion of the whole monastic system by Henry VIII. First, Wolsey was allowed to have a number of small houses of ill conduct, with which to endow his college at Oxford in 1524; then in 1536 came the Dissolution by Act of Parlia-ment of all the smaller houses remaining; finally, one by one, from 1538 to 1540, the surrender to the King's will of the great abbeys which had formed the backbone of English Christianity for so long. Oldest of them all according to legend was Glastonbury, founded in A.D. 63 by a body of apostles who in one story were led by Joseph of Arimathea; in undoubted history an early sanctuary of the British Church, it survived the coming of the Saxons, the ravages of the Danes, the Norman Conquest, and the earthquake of 1276, which threw down the ancient Chapel of St. Michael-on-the-Tor. The Chapel was rebuilt, and though all has gone but the shell of its simple Perpendicular tower, that still stands with its seven niches for statues looking out over the Isle towards the western sea, an enduring memorial to the last abbot, executed at its foot.

From the sad end of English monasticism it is time to turn back to give some account of the later castles and defensive works of the civil power. Skenfrith Castle, Monmouthshire, was originally a motte and bailey work like Rayleigh, and it too came into the hands of Hubert de Burgh, who built the stone keep and curtain-wall with its four corner towers between 1201 and 1205; Mr. Sidney Toy has drawn attention to the fact that the upper floors of the three remaining towers were all on exactly the same level, "as though they had been set out by some delicate and precise instrument". It may be that we have here an example of the skill of that Master Forcinus who was in charge of repairs to Colchester Castle in 1204, when it too was in the custody of Hubert de Burgh. But it seems possible that the heights may have been fixed by direct measurement from the surface of water in the moat, which at Skenfrith washes the foundations of all four walls. The castle was of great importance until the pacification of Wales by Edward I, but by the time of James I a local jury returned that it had been "ruinous and decayed, time out of the memory of man".

Slightly later than Skenfrith is the Pembrokeshire Castle of Cilgerran, whose present buildings are believed to have been built for William Marshal the younger about 1223. The site is however much older, and this may have been the fortress established by Roger de Belesme in 1092, and later strengthened by Gilbert Strongbow. This earlier castle was razed to the ground by the Welsh under Prince Rhys in 1165, then rebuilt, recaptured in 1204 by William Marshal the elder, Earl of Pembroke, lost again in 1213 on Christmas Eve, and finally secured by the younger Marshal some ten years later. By 1387 it was stated to be in a damaged condition, and was perhaps finally dismantled soon after.

Belonging, like Cilgerran, to the reign of Henry III were the walls and towers of Shrewsbury, of which one tower alone now remains, together with a section of the walls. The tower is square and of three stories, standing high above the wall-top overlooking the great loop of the Severn; in its present state it probably consists very largely of repairs done in the fifteenth century, when the civil wars again rendered the Welsh Marches a disturbed and danger-ous district. The campaigns and administrative reforms of Edward I did however secure comparative peace to the greater part of England for more than a century, and this is shown in a new type of castellated mansion, with luxurious dwellings grouped round a courtyard, defended by a moat and by a gatehouse of some strength. An early example of this new type was the house at Boarstall near Brill, Buckinghamshire, which Sir John Handlo had licence to crenellate in 1312; only the gatehouse, known as Boarstall Tower, and the moat now exist, the remains of the mansion having been cleared away in the late eighteenth century. The outer face of the gatehouse was greatly altered in the sixteenth and seventeenth centuries, and large windows were inserted on the inner face, but it is still an interesting work and is rendered somewhat remark-able by its hexagonal corner turrets. Turrets of this form also occur at Berry Pomeroy Castle in Devon, where they are said to be of late fourteenth-century date, and on the great gate of Dunster Castle, Somerset, which is known to have been building as late as 1421, though begun before the turn of the century. It is possible that Boarstall is not the original work carried out for Sir John

Handlo, but the turreted gatehouse is found as early as 1308 at St. Augustine's Abbey, Canterbury. At this period Canterbury fashions were carried across England through the influence of Masters Walter and Thomas of Canterbury, successively masons to the King and designers of the lower and upper Chapels of St. Stephen in the Palace of Westminster.

The square castellated mansion with corner towers was carried a stage further at Shirburn, Oxfordshire, begun in 1377, and was perfected at Bodiam, Sussex, built for Sir Edward Dalyngrigge under a licence dated the 20th October, 1385. From about 1378 French raids on the coast caused extensive fortifications to be undertaken in the South of England and also on the Scottish border. New gates and towers at Canterbury, towers on either side of the Thames below London, a castle at Cooling in Kent for John, Lord Cobham, and a lofty gatehouse at the Archbishop of Canterbury's Castle of Saltwood near Hythe were all designed between 1378 and 1383 by Henry Yevele, the King's Master Mason, while his colleagues William Wynford, mason, and Richard Swift, carpenter, did similar work at Corfe Castle and at Southampton. Later Yevele did extensive works at Canterbury Castle, and he and Wynford jointly were to repair the Castle of Winchester, where Wynford had been engaged by William of Wykeham on the design of his College, and was later, from 1394, to carry out the new Perpendicular nave of the Cathedral. In 1393 a household account roll of Wykeham gives lists which show that while Yevele and Wynford were frequent guests, the Bishop also entertained Sir Edward Dalyngrigge and Sir Richard Abberbury, who eight years earlier had obtained their licences to build the castles of Bodiam and Donnington respec-tively. Dalyngrigge died about 1395, and it seems probable that Bodiam was substantially completed before his death; furthermore, its round corner towers greatly resemble Yevele's known work at Cooling and at Canterbury, while other features suggest details of Wynford's work at Winchester and at New College, Oxford, where the closed quadrangular plan was adopted, though for a different purpose, by 1380. Some ten years earlier Yevele built a tiny quad-rangular college for Lord Cobham's chantry priests at Cobham, Kent, while in 1381 both Yevele and Wynford appear in Wykeham's company at Farnham Castle. One is led to the conclusion that the two masons, the greatest archi-tects of their time, were gradually rationalizing the science of planning, and produced during the last third of the fourteenth century a scheme capable of modification to almost all purposes, from the immense quadrangle of Yevele's London Charterhouse, begun in 1371, for the seclusion of monks devoted to the rigours of solitary life, to the castle of Bodiam, destined to terrorize the French. So successful was this idea that it was widely imitated, and for the rest of the Middle Ages the school, the monastery, the college and the castle grew to resemble each other more and more closely. Apart from their smaller scale, the collegiate buildings at Westbury-on-Trym, with their round corner towers and strong gatehouse, must have borne the closest family likeness to the castles of Shirburn and Bodiam.

During the troubled years of the fifteenth century, however, a new variant of the castle arose, which Dr. Douglas Simpson has termed "the castle of

Livery and Maintenance", distinguished by the possession of a great tower-house, in which the lord could live, secluded from the inconvenient proximity of his own unruly mercenaries. Dr. Simpson has demonstrated the pedigree of this "palatial" type, spreading from France both to the west and eastwards to the Baltic, where it appears at the Castle of the Teutonic Knights at Marien-burg in or soon after 1380. It is certainly remarkable that at Tattershall the leading figure in the building accounts should be one Baldwin Docheman, whose name is as likely to indicate an origin in Hanseatic Germany as in Holland. Whether, as at Tattershall, the tower-house was simply a showy suite of private apartments, or as at Dudley, Nunney, Warkworth and Ashby-de-la-Zouch, a real fortress within a fortress, the removal of the lord from the society of his retainers in the great hall was symptomatic of a fundamental change in society, a loosening of patriarchal bonds and the growth of a new and violent parting between rich and poor, which was to lead to class war. From the purely architectural standpoint Tattershall, begun by Ralph Lord Cromwell in 1433, has some affinity to the turreted gatehouse, and possibly still more to a type of compact quadrangular castle with square corner towers of slight projection which is typical of the North, but goes back to Acton Burnell Castle in Shrop-shire, built in the thirteenth century. It reached its highest development in the hands of John Lewyn, master mason to the Bishops of Durham, and builder of Bolton Castle, Yorkshire, begun about 1377, the finest remaining example of the type. Dr. Simpson has shown with great probability that Lewyn was also the architect of the great donjon at Warkworth, and he was probably responsible for Sheriff Hutton Castle, of the Bolton type, and perhaps for the smaller examples at Lumley, Durham, and Langley, Northumberland. In Ireland, where anarchic conditions prevailed much later than in England, occurs a late but remarkable instance of this type at Kanturk,[1] County Cork, built in the mid-sixteenth century.

By that time in England the progress of artillery had made the lofty walls and towers of the true Middle Ages not only useless but dangerous, and low forts with a wide field of fire for numerous cannon had taken their place. Henry VIII spent a considerable part of the spoils from the sequestrated monasteries upon a series of coastal forts, of which the earliest were designed about 1540 by a German engineer, Stephen von Hashenperg. These forts, of which Deal, Walmer, Sandgate, Camber, Brownsea, St. Mawes and Pendennis are the most famous, protected the south coast; somewhat later the danger zone spread to the north, and soon after Henry VIII's death the fortifications on the Border were greatly strengthened, and a new fort built upon the highest peak of Lindisfarne, between 1548 and 1550. Perched on its crag it has the romantic suggestion of its predecessors, but its blockhouse character foreshadows the modern age; its designer, possibly that Thomas Pettyt who had charge of other Northumbrian fortifications a few years earlier, and who drew the beautiful "Platt of the Lowe Countrye at Calleys", now among the Cotton Manuscripts, in 1545, had a foot in two worlds, and Lindisfarne Castle, posed like Arthur's fortress on the rock of Tintagel, bluntly shoulders the burden of a new day.

---

[1] The only National Trust property in Eire, Kanturk Castle was presented in 1900.

V

THE MANOR HOUSE

By G. M. Young

THE tides of history rise and fall: its currents sweep to and fro: and one of them, in these last years, seems to be eating at the foundations of the English Manor. The elegant simplicity of the three fields, wheat, barley and fallow, raying out from the village clustered round its church; and the reeve, with rod in hand, ordaining what every man should do, and when, has, in the last generation of historic research, been sadly mauled and broken. Few students of history would to-day permit themselves to go further than the cautious admission that, on the whole, the Manor was the commonest type of village organization in England, and this admission must in turn be qualified. Even the Manor is not everywhere the same. Under the type, there are sub-types; the sub-types are not all of a pattern; and the endless diversity of the English landscape is in part the cause, in part the reflexion, of a corresponding diversity in the cultivation of the soil, and so in the social habits of the cultivators. You cannot manage an estate, you cannot work a farm, in Dorset as you might in Suffolk. Neither could you in the Middle Ages. But in the latter part of the fifteenth century—and here again we must not be too rigid, sometimes earlier, sometimes later—we see this variety settling down into a recognizable social pattern, the central figure being—a new word—the landlord, who is commonly also a Justice of the Peace, and lives, in a style becoming his rank, in the Hall, the Manor, or the Place.

The primitive nucleus or cell out of which these houses have grown is the Hall, an oblong room for all purposes, with a chamber at the far end—sometimes raised, and entered by an outer staircase. This is the Bower, where lord and lady slept, the lady plied her needle, and the few treasures of the household were stored. At the nearer end might be a screen to keep the clatter and fumes of the kitchen at bay. Most colleges in Oxford or Cambridge preserve this arrangement still, and, where the Common Room is immediately behind the high table, the plan could with very slight alteration serve for the house of a Norman or Plantagenet knight or franklin. The architectural history of the Manor House can be most simply stated as the growth, and specializing, of the Bower at the expense of the Hall; a development which became possible with the introduction of the ceiling and the chimney. The new second floor provided bedrooms, perhaps opening from a passage, which in the larger houses might be styled a gallery; above the chambers of the family were the garrets for the servants. The Bower became a withdrawing-room, and the Hall was reduced, or divided into rooms for special purposes; a dining-room, a study or Justice Room; in due course, perhaps, a gunroom, a smoking-room, a billiard room. So it has come about that we must needs use the same word

Hall for the Great House of the village, and for the passageway from the front door to the sitting rooms of a suburban villa.

Perhaps the best example, surviving with least change, of the Hall or Place of that age, is Great Chalfield in Wiltshire. The founder, Thomas Tropenell, was known to his neighbours as a "perillous covetous man", a description borne out by the fresco portrait still remaining on the wall of the house h ebuilt for himself, in the loop of a stream, and so, if need arose, defensible. In course of time this Hall became a farmhouse. But, happily, it was always well cared for and maintained. In the twenties of the last century a pupil of Pugin's made measured drawings of the structure and its details, from which injured or missing parts could be restored; and by a final stroke of good fortune, the great Ledger Book in which Tropenell entered the title deeds of his numerous pro- perties came unexpectedly to light some forty years ago and now lies in its oaken box in the hall of Tropenell's Manor House.

With Great Chalfield, though on a lesser scale, may be ranged the fifteenth- century stone-built Manor—Chilmark quarries, from which Salisbury Cathedral was built, are within a short haul—called Little Clarendon, at Dinton in Wiltshire, and Westwood[1] by Bradford-on-Avon. Of the same period, but in a different style, is Stoneacre at Otham in Kent, in the half- timber characteristic of a forest area, a beautifully compact example of the Hall. As a third may be added Bradley Manor at Newton Abbot, in Devon, where the carving on the screen indicates a new influence, radiating from Hampton Court—the influence of Italy—while the late Gothic windows, in contrast with the meagre lighting of an earlier age, begin to point forward to the broad illumination of the Tudor galleries.

At Chalfield we are still in the age when men took their bows and arrows with them when they went reaping, and a sudden barking of the dogs would set all hands to bar the gates and man the walls against the Beggars, disbanded retainers from the beaten side, Red Rose or White, in the last battle, some in rags and some in tags, and some in silken gowns, the plunder of some un- defended Manor House. Even under the Tudor Peace, we may read of old grudges fought out with bows and shotguns from the tower of the church or the windows of the Hall, while the tithingman, white rod in hand, lent counten- ance to the proceedings, and the Justice, hurriedly summoned, rode up with his constables to bind everybody over to keep the peace, and send recalcitrants to Assizes for a misdemeanour, or to Star Chamber for a riot.

But with the close of the dynastic wars, the necessity of defence, as a thing of course, rapidly passed away. Comparing one of our few surviving Manor Houses from the Middle Ages with one of the many that were built in, and have stayed unchanged from, Tudor times, we have the impression of a country- side sunning itself in a long awaited peace. There is more light and air and room; broader galleries, more curiously devised gardens. Of this, which we may perhaps call pure Tudor, deliberately comfortable, consciously secure, and availing itself to the full of the cheapness and facility of brick, there is to be seen an excellent example at Eastbury Manor, Barking: now the Museum

---

[1] Protected but not owned by the National Trust.

43 Great Chalfield, Wiltshire: the Manor House and Church, from a drawing by J. C. Buckler

44 Eastbury Manor House, Barking: the Courtyard Side

45 Stoneacre, Otham, Kent

46 Kanturk Castle, County Cork, Eire

47 Lyveden New Build, Northamptonshire, by Sir Thomas Tresham

48   Wilderhope Manor House, Wenlock Edge, Shropshire

of the Corporation. This is of the mid-century. A generation later comes Wilderhope Manor, Shropshire, where we see what opportunities an upper storey and a ceiling gave to craftsmen in two arts—in plaster and in the contrivance of staircases. Sometimes, when the main beam of the hall was too near the roof, the problem was beyond the builder's powers; going to bed at Stoneacre must have been an adventure, fruitful in broken heads and black eyes. Wilderhope, stone-built, is an outlier of the Cotswold style, which lingered so long that it almost bridged the interim between the latest Gothic in the mid-seventeenth century and the first glimmerings of the Gothic revival in the early eighteenth. Packwood House in Warwickshire is earlier but has received additions in red brick of Restoration date. Thorington, in Suffolk, a timber-framed house in the local style, though somewhat late in time, is, in feeling, pure Elizabethan.

But already a breath from Italy is coming up this way, bringing with it some feeling for balance and proportion and sometimes spurring the native craftsman into a bewildered extravagance of fancy. This, which might be described as Italian not quite domiciled, or native baroque, furnishes its most striking examples (the epithet is in places uncomfortably right) in houses built to a grander fashion than the resources of the squire could compass. East Riddlesden shows the stubbornness of the Gothic, neither quite rejecting nor quite admitting the new style; and Lyveden New Build in Northamptonshire is one of three buildings by Thomas Tresham, in whose hands it was rather a fancy to be indulged than an idea to be developed. That is Jacobean, and it will pass. What will remain is a certain, almost classical, precision of touch; the gift of craftsmen, unnamed, innumerable; of men who learnt from Webb what Webb had learnt from Inigo, and Inigo had drawn from the fountain head in Vicenza; and at Thorney Abbey House[1] we have Webb's own hand.

But these changes are, as it were, laid down on a structural continuity, reflecting the continuity of rural life and its necessary institutions, the administration of justice, the relief of the poor, and the cultivation of the soil. At St. John's Jerusalem in Kent we have a noble example of persistent habitation—a Preceptory of the thirteenth century complete with chapel and half-moat, which has received only one substantial alteration, in red brick of the early eighteenth century. But there are scores of Manor Houses where careful study will disclose the primitive nucleus; perhaps a yeoman's house of the fifteenth century, ceiled and enlarged in the sixteenth; brick-faced with stone quoins, and its internal dispositions rearranged, lighted and, we may say, civilized in the seventeenth, by a prosperous sheep-master who has married the last scion of an old family, and means to have everything about him as handsome as good building, good joinery and good tapestry, fine windows and perhaps a timely gift to the Heralds in return for a new-engrossed Pettigrew, can make it. Longleat and Hatfield, Wilton and Raby, are for the great. But even the greatest, warned by the fates of Somerset and Norfolk and more than one Earl of Essex, are coming to see that, if there is little safety at Court, there is much strength in Parliament, and that what Parliament will do depends very much

---

[1] Protected but not owned by the National Trust.

upon what the Manor Houses think. It was the Manor Houses that sentenced Strafford, and it was the Manor Houses that restored the King.

Indeed in the days of difficult communication, and an isolated, and strongly characterized, local life, we may think of the Manor Houses as being at once the centres of political activity, of justice and administration, and, in the remoter shires, as anticipating the future railway stations and hotels. Of the life lived in them, say from the Restoration to the general levelling of habits in the Victorian Age, we may form the most varied picture, which will yet not be more varied than the original. The name, and notion, of Squire first meets us in the reign of Anne, and then in the writings of urban humourists, to whom the appearance of one of those strange creatures wearing strange clothes and often speaking a strange dialect, was a source of constant entertainment; and, as the Squire was commonly a Tory, with a leaning to the House of Stuart and maybe to the Church of Rome, he was not likely to be treated with partiality by Whig writers in the days of Whig ascendancy and Whig patronage. Transmitted to Macaulay the picture was repainted with heightened colour and deeper shades. But anyone who has studied the decoration of the Manor Houses, turned over the books in their libraries, handled their furniture and plate and read what has come down of their correspondence, knows well enough that it would be most unsafe to draw a composite portrait of the Old English Gentleman from Squire Western and Sir Hildebrand Osbaldeston, even if Sir Roger de Coverley was thrown in to soften the tones. Doubtless they all had something in common: the habit of being obeyed, of living generously, of thinking well of themselves and their order. But the identity goes little farther, and Quarter Sessions and Assizes, the county election and the opening day of the hunt, probably brought together as great a variety of characters as ever stood against a single background.

"Barbarians?" said the Epirote king when he saw the Roman legions drawn out; "there is nothing barbaric in their order of battle." From about 1660 to 1820, with a higher range from 1720 to 1780, we see the English art of domestic architecture, minor architecture, at its fullest and most exquisite development. The Gothic idea had gradually died out, though it is often interesting to observe, in barns and cottages of the stone country, some late remaining touch of an earlier time, a coping, an unexpected mullion; the crude exuberance of the Italianate had been subdued; a conscious taste was forming, critical and selective. And eclectic, because there is hardly a detail or a proportion in the English Manor House of the late seventeenth and eighteenth centuries which cannot be derived from Italian prototypes. Yet nothing, unless it be the village church, is more characteristic of the English scene than the Manor House; perhaps because nothing realizes so completely that grafting of Renaissance culture on English stock which is the key to so much in the history of our civilization, "the eternal craving of the North for the South". First came security: the house must be able to stand up to wind and weather, quarrelsome neighbours or discontented peasants. These things assured, we thought of comfort next: and last of all, in Sir Henry Wotton's word, delight. It is not enough for the house to be warm in winter and cool in summer, with a pleasant garden of flowers and herbs, and a fine sporting prospect from the windows. It must be good to look at as well. It must mean something to those who catch a sight of it down a glade in its surrounding park. And if the Manor Houses of the Elizabethan and Jacobean times often look as if they were designed to shelter and display the conscious pride and power of new wealth, those of the later, the Golden Age, are hardly ever pretentious, never startling, never obtrusive, the natural living places of people who were quietly satisfied with themselves, and knew how to strike a just balance between art and comfort, sport and culture, dignity and use.

A fine example of what might be called the early Golden Age is Batemans near Burwash, in Sussex, dated 1634, and for many years the home of Rudyard Kipling. Even more notable, perhaps, for its disclosure of a yeoman's taste and style, is Owletts at Cobham. It is simple, even heavy, in build. But:

> A knight of Cales
> A squire of Wales
>   And a lord of the north countree:
> A yeoman of Kent
> With a half year's rent
>   Will buy them out all three,

and the door of Owletts opens to display an interior as spacious and splendid as any great house could show. The staircase at Princes Risborough Manor is slightly older: the house, as we see it, is red brick of William and Mary's time. Hambleden Manor[1] (1604) is Jacobean by date: Culham Court[1] (1770) is near the end of the great age: Kenricks[1] is Georgian of the centre.

But great art—and this art of domestic architecture is the one in which we can fairly claim to stand supreme—is not produced by instinct, or some happy, casual, combination of pattern-books and climate, though both had their share in the evolution of the eighteenth-century Manor House. Something of the spirit which in the Middle Ages set parishes vying with each other in richer windows, ampler naves, and more numerous angels supporting more glorious roofs, returned to direct the ambition of landowners and animate the practice of their builders. In 1728 James Gibbs—an Aberdeen Catholic who had studied at Rome and was to enrich London, Oxford and Cambridge with three of their finest buildings—published for the use and guidance of the nobility and gentry, his Book of Architecture; and one sentence in the preface carries us straight into the eighteenth century world of taste, of "order, regularity and refinement". If, as someone has said, architecture is music in stone, the eighteenth-century Manor House—and beside the Hall we must set the Dower House and the Parsonage—might be described as the heroic couplet rendered in brick, with stone quoins for the rhymes. Here are Gibbs's own words:

"Some, for want of better Helps, have unfortunately put into the hands of common workmen, the management of buildings of considerable expense; which, when finished, they have had the mortification to find condemned by persons of Tast, to that degree that sometimes they have been pull'd down, at least alter'd at a greater charge than would have procured better

[1] Protected but not owned by the National Trust.

advice from an able Artist; or if they have stood, they have remained lasting Monuments of the Ignorance or Parsimoniousness of the Owners, or (it may be) of a wrong-judged Profuseness."

But the "able artist", we must remember, was not confined to the Place or the Hall. The wealthy citizen was pushing out into the country and calling for a habitation suitable to his state. Aspiring little boroughs were rebuilding their town halls, and commissioning new market houses. And the builder who had finished his work under the eye of a trained architect at the Great House, was always ready to put his experience and his pattern-books at the disposal of the merchant and lawyer, the doctor, the clothiers in the woollen town, or the canons in the close. Thus there came about that remarkable diffusion and uniformity of style which at a glance identifies, it may be the Custom House or it may be the surgery, as Georgian. Hyde's House at Dinton, which shows the influence of Wren, is, none the less, of purely rustic conception. Holt, twenty years earlier, gives rather the impression of a town house which has parted from its moorings and come to anchor in the country; and indeed the clothing towns of the west hold houses still which vie in grace and dignity with any manor.

Many reasons could be, and have been given for the rapid decline of architectural skill and judgement in the early nineteenth century, and it is not at all impossible that some change of taste may bring into notice work over-looked to-day as merely Victorian or merely Gothic Revival. We can hardly suppose that craftsmen who had worked for Decimus Burton at Tunbridge Wells or Papworth at Cheltenham, could not have built Manor Houses as good as any of their predecessors, if their patrons had been so minded. Perhaps they were not; and it is difficult to imagine a Victorian proprietor pulling down a lodge or a dairy because his more critical neighbours had condemned it. In the clamour of First-pointed, Second-pointed, Baronial, Lombardic, choice was confused and tradition lost, while the new towns were drawing more and more of the old building crafts into themselves, and degrading what they drew. In Wightwick Manor, with its pre-Raphaelite associations, we have a characteristic example of a Victorian residence in the manorial style. But the Manor House had been much more than that, and when it was no longer needed as a place of hospitality to travellers or a seat of justice and administra-tion, its object was served, and its end had come—unless indeed a changing world brings it new purposes to fulfil.

49 Hyde's House, Dinton, Wiltshire

50 Chadwich Manor House, Worcestershire

51   Little Moreton Hall, Cheshire

52   Speke Hall, Lancashire: the Hall. From the water colour by Joseph Nash

VI

THE COUNTRY HOUSE

By James Lees-Milne

The free, fair homes of England!
Long, long, in hut and hall,
May hearts of native proof be reared
To guard each hallowed wall!

What to the National Trust is a comparatively recent and very perplexing problem presented little anxiety to Mrs. Hemans's admonitory muse just over one hundred years ago. Within the last ten years or so changing economic and social conditions have aroused a wide national interest in the great historic country houses which for long had been the comfortable concern of a few privileged families. The first person to call public attention to the dangers confronting their future was the late Lord Lothian in a speech he made at an Annual Meeting of the National Trust in 1934. Of the larger country houses the Trust at that time owned but two, namely Montacute and Barrington Court, both in Somerset, whereas to-day it owns seventeen, and protects by means of restrictive covenants five others. Of these seventeen owned nine are still inhabited, at least partially, by the families of their donors, one is let to a private tenant in the usual way, four are now purely show places, one is let to an institution, whereas the future use of the remaining two is as yet uncertain. All are to be open to the public at stated times.

For centuries now the great houses of Britain, with their infinite appeal and varied associations, have epitomized many aspects of this island's history, and they are at long last venerated as the traditional archives of our past and present. Their changing future lies in our hands, nor with a little positive imagination need they become moribund. The reasons why we so jealously cherish them, though not hard to seek, are not so easy to define. For the purpose of this chapter, country houses may be said to impart five particular aspects. In their very fabric they provide the study of an evolutionary vernacular architecture: in their furnishings and collections of virtu the study of the domestic arts generally: in their surroundings and grounds the study of horticulture and silviculture: in their peculiar spirit the study of field sports, so beloved by the British all the world over: and in their associations the study of social history from distant down to the most recent times.

As for a pure architectural specimen—the pedant's will-o'-the-wisp—there is rarely any such thing and possibly the greatest charm to most visitors lies in the quiet development of styles and tastes that individual English houses so usually display. Adherence to a strict chronology is therefore apt to be misleading. Yet for our purpose we shall arbitrarily begin with—broadly speaking —the Renaissance and end with pre-Raphaelitism. There must necessarily be a good deal of dovetailing of age with style for whereas Rufford Old Hall is the older of the two country houses in point of time, Lindisfarne Castle represents the earlier inhabited type (although its interior is by chance almost wholly of the most recent times, being the work of Sir Edwyn Lutyens). Lindisfarne was actually erected in Edward VI's reign when defence considerations were generally receding from domestic architecture, as a sea coast fortress against possible Scottish and French invasion. In 1539 an Order in Council had provided for a chain of such castles where "all havens should be fensed with bulwarks and blokehouses" (this word has a familiar ring) along the north-eastern coast. It springs its grey bulk against the Northumbrian sky from the steep formation of Holy Island so as to be almost indistinguishable from its rocky foundation. Rufford Old Hall (c. 1500) is likewise distinctly medieval in conception, being of half timber construction, complete with open hall and angel hammer-beam roof of true Gothic detail, oriel window, raised dais and screens passage, only here with the curious "spere" disposition indigenous to Lancashire, and the monstrous moveable screen that excites exacerbated controversy amongst the experts.

In this sequence there naturally come other black-and-white structures in which examples the National Trust is fortunately rich, for Little Moreton Hall (1559-80) and Speke Hall (1530-98) are both well known. Here we have two houses that grew to completion over several decades so that it is awkward to assign to the respective additions their precise dates, where these are not recorded on the façades nor to be diagnosed by means of moulds, the surest guides to Tudor structural development. In both cases however the results achieve harmonious wholes. Moreton suggests a fantastic overgrown doll's house, Speke a more adult residence. In both houses the mediaeval open hall is almost gone, yet both are still moated, both built round a central open court and still integrally Gothic in their conception. This form of timber post and plaster-filled building was extremely common in Tudor England and was not peculiar to the old forest areas, as John Leland, King Henry VIII's itinerant surveyor throughout the whole country, testifies. Nor was it confined of course to the dwellings of the poorest subjects in the land. Spanish visitors in Queen Mary's reign were amazed at the apparent paucity of the material. "These English", they declared, "have their houses made of sticks and dirt, but they fare commonly so well as the King."

Yet in the essentially stone districts this is the material we usually find at an even earlier date, as at Knole[1] which assumed its present shape between the years 1454-86. Here the defensive element which still lingers is traced in the vast perimeter of outer walls, enclosing, themselves originally almost impregnable and entered by a gatehouse, a series of inner courts, so as rather to resemble a medieval town than our conception of a nobleman's palace. The Knole disposition reflects likewise the monastic development, which is even better, for it is directly exemplified at Lacock Abbey, a typical instance of a Tudor gentleman's residence based upon the spoils of the Church. Lacock moreover, with its range of styles over seven centuries, shows in Sir William Sharington's

[1] Lord Sackville has announced his intention of handing Knole to the care of the National Trust.

53   Speke Hall, Lancashire: the Gatehouse. From the water colour by
Joseph Nash

contribution the purest Italian as opposed to Flemish Renaissance work, and dates from Edward VI's reign. Coughton Court again is a compromise of the two developments and the two materials with its defensive Henry VII gatehouse of stone and two projecting domestic wings of half timber.

In Barrington Court (1514/20), integrally Gothic but burgeoning early Renaissance detail, we have a similar exuberance in adornment to Moreton and Speke, only in stone. Directly inspired by Lord Daubeny, fresh from the Field of the Cloth of Gold, it affords one of the earliest instances of "archi/ tecture", for it shows symmetry and style. It is an attempted work of art, divorced from the defensive element, and purely domestic. With Montacute (1580/1600) the Renaissance has by now truly taken hold in plan and execu/ tion. The building is even attributed with some probability to the name of an actual architect, as we understand the term, the elusive John Thorpe. The great hall has lost its open roof, the screens are emasculated. Although the long gallery remains, the window pediments and other detail evince that the classical has been adopted. Montacute is a thorough Elizabethan, transi/ tional without being vulgar, lavish, exquisite and successful, which is more than can be said of many of its great contemporaries such as Burghley and Wollaton Hall. It is in fact almost a work of art.

To strictly Jacobean Blickling (1616/28), just a generation younger, the name of Robert Lyminge, master builder of Hatfield, is authentically ascribed. Blickling is not even entirely free from Gothic influence, certainly not from Elizabethan exuberances. There is a fancifulness about its red brick gables and its strapwork conceits in stone upon the façade, but there is no longer a great hall, and the great gallery under the eaves has succumbed to a room of more manageable proportions on the first floor. The next generation is repre/ sented by Carolean Swakeleys[1] (1638), showing yet further development towards compactness of plan and restraint of detail. In Commonwealth Coleshill (1650) the peak of purist classicism is reached. The great name of Inigo Jones is associated with this distinct work of art, carried out by his disciple, the amateur Roger Pratt. Here the very remnants of Gothicism and the pseudo/classicism of the Jacobeans have been discarded. Jones derived his inspiration direct from Vitruvius and Palladio, and drilled it to the tune of symmetry and the Orders. For about the first time in English architecture the *piano nobile* is introduced, as Celia Fiennes visiting Coleshill in King William III's reign was surprised to notice. "Most of ye offices are partly underground." "The entrance of ye house", she comments, "is an ascent of severall steps", indicating a complete departure from the traditional construc/ tion of the principal rooms upon ground level. The hall without screens is the central feature, the doors to it forming the axis to the whole house, whereas a double flight of "spacious and handsome staires runs up and meetes on the landing place".

The great age of Wren saw little development in country house architecture upon that of Jones. Only two or three country houses are with any certainty attributed to the prolific Sir Christopher himself. The National Trust owns

[1] Protected, but not owned, by the National Trust.

one example of his school in Gunby Hall, Lincolnshire, an unsophisticated provincial version in red brick, dating from William III's reign. A perfect example of pure Queen Anne is Bradbourne,[1] also in brick, where, inside, the delicate treatment of the wainscoting and stair furniture marks the advent of the joiner's art. Here is English gauged and rubbed brickwork at its most refined. The walls are of pinkish stock with panels of mauve, green, yellow and buff, and dressings of bright red brick. By the second quarter of the eighteenth century the great era of country house building is in full swing, of the Castle Howards, the Holkhams and the Ditchleys, examples of those great architects, Vanburgh, Kent and Gibbs, some of whose creations the Trust has yet to acquire.

Wallington (actually dating from 1688) affords a fine example of the 1740 rococo period that succeeded the baroque, in its great saloon with white scroll stucco reliefs upon a coved ceiling of egg blue ground and walls of original Neapolitan yellow, a room "of good height" and "most elegantly proportioned", as Arthur Young observed during a visit in 1768. The rococo period was followed by extravagant interludes of Chinese and Gothic Revival tastes, of which latter Horace Walpole's protégé, Sanderson Miller, has left a sample in his hall and garden archway at Lacock (1754). This leads to the unchallenged reign of Robert Adam, one of whose very earliest works was Hatchlands (1759). This house, whose uneventful exterior was entirely subordinated to its interior, is interesting in showing the more robust virtuosity of Adam's astonishing genius under the direct influence of his Roman studies and the recent discoveries of Herculaneum and Pompeii, as opposed to the influence of the Grecian studies of "Athenian" Stuart and Revett. Of Revett's Grecian, ism a very early example is his portico at West Wycombe Park. This house coeval with Hatchlands, is however mainly the work of an amateur disciple of Adam, the dilettante, cognoscente, Sir Francis Dashwood, who made striking use of those ersatz materials lately brought into the architectural markets, namely artificial stones and stucco papers.

Adam had innumerable followers and imitators of scarcely less distinction than himself, such as Thomas Leverton, Joseph Bonomi, Henry Holland, Cockerell, Crunden and Sir John Soane. The Trust has, as yet, no examples of their works, but we must remember that it is rarely able to pick upon a favoured type of property at a chosen moment. Rather the Trust is faced with the immediate acceptance or rejection of whatever may come its way, usually unforewarned. Of greater renown perhaps than these architects are the Wyatt family and so late as the year of Waterloo Geoffrey Wyatt (alias Wyatt, ville) proved how traditional and classical he could be at Dinton Park (1815). Since it is no longer fashionable to depreciate the mid, Victorians, of Sir Charles Barry's work we may safely admire what is probably one of the last examples of severe Palladianism in the elevations of Cliveden (1850).

To estimate our seventeenth, and eighteenth, century ancestors' precise response to and judgement of aesthetics and the arts is often a difficult and hazardous

[1] Protected, but not owned by the National Trust.

54   Knole, Sevenoaks, Kent

55 Knole, Kent: the Green Court

56 Knole, Kent: the Hall and Screen

57　Montacute, Somerset: one of the Terrace Pavilions

58　Montacute, Somerset: the Hall Screen

59   Montacute, Somerset: a Gable, and part of the Terrace

undertaking. The more we read their impressions in journals and memoirs the more bewildering, arbitrary and whimsical do they seem. Old inventories such as the famous Lumley Castle or Standon Lordship ones are frankly non-committal in this respect. Samuel Pepys who may be said to represent the man-in-the-street's point of view and who visited Swakeleys in 1665 was far more taken with his host's relic of a dried blackamoor boy in a box than with the "window cases, door cases and chimneys of all the house" in marble. His contemporary, John Evelyn, a connoisseur and man of taste in the eyes of his world, is equally disappointing and tends merely to be comparative. He likens the gardens at Cliveden to Italian ones, ending with the comment that they are "august and stately" merely. Lord Burlington, the great virtuoso, assessed the correctitude of architecture in accordance with its undeviating adherence to Palladian rules and admired Kent as an artist in oil painting—which he wasn't—as wilfully as he despised Hogarth, who was. Sir Francis Dashwood's judgement of painting may be gauged by the mediocre quality of the old masters he collected at West Wycombe. Not until Horace Walpole's notes on the arts do we get serious attempts at criticism and his to our minds are more subjective than exact. Others again condemned in no measured terms what we frankly fail to find offensive, like the antiquarian Lord Torrington, who arbitrarily dismissed much that we account pretty as "ugly" and Gunby Hall as "a most melancholy place". All that Bishop Pococke found to admire at Coleshill in 1757 and William Cobbett in 1825 were the one the water pipes that fed the garden fountain, the other the contented faces of the farm labourers on the estate. From their recorded impressions then we do not get far. We can fortunately judge their accidentally inerrable good taste in furniture, porcelain, or silver, from what they have bequeathed us, but we are quite in the dark as to the standards that dictated this good taste to them.

In early Tudor times the houses of the nobility were lacking in practically everything that constitutes comfort. The floor of the great hall was usually of hard trampled clay, strewn maybe with rushes (occasionally impregnated by the more sensuous with sweet-smelling herbs or saffron). These were swept away once or twice a month, together with the dirt, fleas, dogs' ordure and remnants of old meat and bones. The furniture of rude oak was sparse indeed. William Harrison, writing *circa* 1587, remarks upon the floors paved with plaster of Paris as an innovation. The walls are, he says, hung with arras or tapestry or painted cloths, depicting hunting scenes, herbs, beasts or knots. More often the plaster fillings of the walls of the lesser gentry are stencilled over in some conventional pattern, the design overlapping the timber beams that would be whitewashed and not, except possibly in the poorest cottages, be revealed. By late Elizabethan times wainscoting, garishly coloured, was very common. Large oak beds had replaced the straw pallets, pillows the hard log to rest the head upon, and down mattresses and fine linen were introduced. Sir John Harington had certainly designed the first water-closet complete with goldfish, nonchalantly swimming in a glass tank above, like the pensive Selima's prey unmindful of an impending fate. But this invention, if carried out at all, was confined to royal use exclusively. Stoves began to be made "now and then to sweat in as occasions and need shall require it". Glass to windows was universal and had replaced the linen steeped in oil of Henry VII's time, and chimneys were substituted for the open hearth in the middle of the hall. "And yet", the hardened Harrison growls, "our gentles complain of rheums, catarrhs, etc." in spite of these luxuries.

By James I's time furniture was less scanty. The bulbous court cupboards, the long refectory tables, genteelly covered with carpets, were in general use. Chairs were however still hard and unupholstered. By Cromwellian times they were seated and backed in leather and by the end of the century often with wicker cane. Charles II's reign saw cushions in lavish gros point and squabs are frequently mentioned in the Blickling inventory of 1699. At Knole there is the famous silver furniture of this time. Even so, furniture was still fairly sparse and Celia Fiennes at Coleshill notices but "few pictures in the house only over doores and chimneys". Until the end of the seventeenth century privacy in a household was held of little account. Stock locks on doors were a luxury, passages were infrequent, which explain the great four-posters with their heavy crewel work hangings that would snugly enclose the master and mistress reading out loud to each other, maybe *Paradise Regained*, from a candle or rush light set at the bedhead, undisturbed by the rest of the family's to and fro. Sir Ralph Verney writing to his wife in 1645 gives a clear sketch of the interior of Claydon at this time: "The odd things in the roome my mother keept herself, the iron closet, the little roome between her bed's head and the backstairs, the little and great Fripperies [hanging closets for gowns], your owne greene wrought velvet furniture, the red velvet furniture, the looking-glasses (there should be at least four), leather carpets for the dininge and drawinge rooms [probably wall hangings], the stooles with nailes guilt, the great cabanet like yours, the tapestry, the great branch candlestick, all such wrought worke as my mother had from London and was not finished, the book of martirs and other bookes in the withdrawing-room, the preserving room, the spicery with furnaces, brewing vessels, and a brass skillet; plat left for the children's use, all the lockes that are loose in the closet." All—to Sir Ralph indeed—casual furnishings, their good workmanship taken for granted and their utilitarian value alone esteemed.

Art for art's sake was first properly understood in England by Charles I whose great collection of pictures indicated his scholarship and discernment. At his death his pictures and furniture were left to his household servants in part payment of arrears of wages. Colonel Hutchinson, the regicide, from the same art-loving motives as the King purchased £2,000 worth of the royal pictures which were promptly forfeited at the time of his disgrace. Such love of art was unusual among Roundheads and even the Colonel was not above ordering out of Puritanic zeal a Nottinghamshire vicar to deface all the religious paintings and glass in his Church. Until the eighteenth century it is questionable whether the English gentry for the most part looked upon pictures other than furnishings and portrait paintings than we do photography. Streater's noble mural paintings at Swakeleys were surely commissioned as a decorative rather than artistic feature to the stairwell, the artist being paid for them by the square yard. Lady Sussex treated Vandyke in a manner no Bond Street photographer of our day would submit to. In Queen Anne's reign Addison makes Sir Roger de Coverley, that ubiquitous lowbrow, conduct the spectator round his portrait gallery. The worthy knight compares the fashions of yesterday with to-day. "My grandmother appears as if she stood in a large Drum, whereas the ladies now walk as if they were in a go-cart." This other ancestor "is said to be the first that made love by squeezing the hand", and so he continues, but there are no references by either party to the quality of the paintings themselves. Sir Roger adopts the same attitude to his furniture, which we may safely guess was uniformly good. "The walls of his Great Hall are covered with the horns of several kinds of deer that he has killed in the chase, which he thinks the most valuable furniture of his house."

The retrograde attitude to art after King Charles I's death was due to the triumph of Puritanism, but by the second quarter of the eighteenth century art for art's sake takes firm hold under the patronage of the great Whig lords, Burlington, Pembroke and Leicester, a symptom chiefly to be attributed to the versatile genius of William Kent. Thereafter, of course, a catholic interest in the arts is in fullest spate. The eighteenth century was moreover the golden age of patronage. Not only were the best artists like Wilson and Gainsborough patronized by the nobility, but artists themselves, like Sir Joshua Reynolds, were acclaimed the arbiters of taste who laid down severe canons from which artistic developments dare not digress. Patrons themselves became artists for, above all, the eighteenth century was the heyday of the dilettante amateur, as instanced by Lord Buckinghamshire's voluminous correspondence upon the improvements he personally was designing and conducting at Blickling. Designers of furniture were munificently recompensed for their pains by the great. Kent was commissioned to furnish Coleshill, Robert Adam Hatchlands. Ince and Mayhew, the Chippendales, Mrs. Hepplewhite and Sheraton filled the great houses with their chairs and tables. Lord and squire vied with one another in acquiring the silver of Paul Lamerie, Wedgwood's Etrurian pottery, the porcelain of Mr. Sprimont's Chelsea factory, of Derby, Worcester or Nantgarw. Each successive decade bore an evolutionary artistic stamp upon its furnishings even beyond the 1840's and Pugin's wild Gothic extravagancies. Alas, the crash was brought about by the superabundant wealth and the concomitant cheap taste of the mid-nineteenth century, when we find Professor Hungerford Pollen perpetrating the most monstrous decorative injustices to the great library at Blickling. Yet the flickering torch of cultural sensibility was not wholly extinct. The revolutionary pre-Raphaelite brotherhood reaped a very positive harvest of country house decoration under the reign of Pauline, Lady Trevelyan, at Wallington, in the remote Northumberland fastnesses.

Thus we are left in our own astonishingly barren and barbarous century with some of the past centuries' choicest collections, on the grand scale as at Knole, on a lesser but more intimate scale as at Wallington and Gunby Hall.

The gardens replete with borders of homely and exotic flowers in which so many old houses, such as Barrington Court are enshrined, and which to many visitors afford these houses' most popular feature, are of comparatively recent revival. It is often forgotten how much is owed for the present condition of English gardens to the late William Robinson and Miss Gertrude Jekyll, the authors and protagonists of the herbaceous border. Our ancestors did not relish too splendid a profusion of flowers. Until the early nineteenth century old prints reveal the great country houses standing stark in open parks with the deer grazing up to the very windows. Francis Bacon in his famous essay on gardens was about the last to give much space to flowers for their own sakes, notwithstanding which he dwells pretty constantly upon herbs. A medieval garden would disappoint twentieth-century flower lovers less than a seventeenth- or eighteenth-century garden, as illuminated missals of these earlier centuries indicate. Even so, the mediaeval gardener cultivated plants first and foremost because of their medicinal and healing properties. Between the reigns of Henry IV and Henry VIII fruits and vegetables had been neglected. William Harrison writes in 1587: "It is a world also to see how many strange herbs, plants and unusual fruits are daily brought unto us from the Indies, Americas, Taprobane, Canary Isles and all parts of the world"—the inevitable products of Elizabethan ventures into new continents. In one garden Harrison has seen 300 to 400 medicinal herbs of foreign extraction. Orchards, he says, have within the past forty years specialized in apple, plum, pear, walnut and filbert trees; also in apricots, almonds, peaches and figs. In a gardener's bill preserved at Knole and dated 1692, all these vegetable products are accounted everyday matters, as are "sweet yerbs, pawsley, sorrill, spinnig, spruts, leeks, sallat, horse rydish, jerusalem hawty-chorks".

As a relic of the medieval garden we have at Little Moreton within and without the moat the raised mound, an artificial construction that bore an arbour upon its summit. Bacon enjoins: "At the end of both the side grounds I would have a mount of some pretty height, leaving the wall of the enclosure breast-high, to look abroad into the fields." A slightly later example is the coeval convention of the raised terrace at Montacute. These justly famed Jacobean gardens must be accepted with caution. The east forecourt with its pavilions and cupolas connected by balustraded retaining walls are contemporary and unique. The north garden, where is the raised Jacobean terrace, otherwise dates from the late eighteenth century, with its beautiful pool balustrading and orangery. Here in Jacobean times, instead of closely scythed lawns were probably knots, or figures in box, filled in the middle with divers coloured earths or chipped marbles, if not an elaborate kitchen-cum-ornamental garden with plenty of trained espaliers. These knots were the prevailing vogue and as such despised by Bacon who calls them "but toys; you may see as good sights many times in tarts". Whereas orangeries date from the late seventeenth century at earliest, Jacobean houses often had roofed but open arcaded corridors with loggias upon terraces as at Bramshill,[1] whereon the ladies exercised themselves with the return of spring, when the long gallery was considered too confined.

A great feature of the seventeenth-century country house was the topiary garden in yew, of which that at Levens by the Frenchman, Beaumont, is a very

---

[1] Protected, but not owned, by the National Trust.

60 Blickling Hall, Norfolk

61 Lacock Abbey, Wiltshire

64   Little Clarendon, Dinton, Wiltshire

63   Rufford Old Hall, Lancashire

65　Coleshill, Berkshire, by Sir Roger Pratt

66　Coleshill: the Staircase Hall

famous example. No better example of its kind can be found than that at Packwood, dating from the Commonwealth. It illustrates the Sermon on the Mount (still the raised mound), representing the figures of Our Lord, the disciples and the multitude in yew. At Packwood also there is a Carolean square garden with raised terrace, corner gazebos and gate piers in brick, contemporary wrought-iron gates and even niches for the bee skeps in the terrace wall.

Towards the end of the century was felt the influence of Lenôtre, who never came to England, in the straight, formal intersecting rides usually through pleached lime and hornbeam bosquets, and in rectangular canals. England never achieved under Messrs. London and Wise the continental magnificence or scale of the Versailles or Beloeil gardens, but Wrest and Bramham Park do not fall far short of them. Kip's views of this period are familiar: formality of line spreading far beyond the box parterres into the kitchen gardens with their serried regiments of fruit trees and into the straight avenued parks. The National Trust has something of this style in the formal garden at Blickling, encompassed by a surrounding raised terrace and ha-ha. At the ends of these straight rides and at the intersections vast plinthed urns were placed. Bridge-man, the inventor of the ha-ha, was the first to break down the formal style by embracing the outlying country in his garden scheme where, in the words of Thomson, "The bursting prospect spreads immense around", so that the eye may roam:

> "To where the broken landscape by degrees
> Ascending, roughens into rigid hills."

We all know how William Kent developed the informal-formal garden at Chiswick with the slogan "Nature abhors a straight line". With him the mania for temples and grottos arose and at Cliveden there are two of this date by Thomas Archer and Giacomo Leoni. Evelyn visited Cliveden in 1679 and was immensely struck with the gardens. "The place", he wrote, "alto-gether answers the most poetical description that can be made of solitude, precipice, prospect, or whatever can contribute to a thing so very like their imaginations." This description is a foretaste of the mid-eighteenth century romantic style of landscape garden that followed hard upon Kent's groves and grottos and which is so admirably preserved in Mr. Henry Hoare's own layout at Stourhead.[1] Here we have a chain of lakes embosomed in mature trees, hardwoods intermixed with conifers, a precise ordered disorder, nature still well under man's control. On the shores of the lakes stands a Pantheon con-taining statuary and sarcophagi, a hermitage and a chasmic rocaille grot with Father Neptune leaning over a clear pool of spring-water under appropriate stalactites. Nor is the couplet by Alexander Pope, engraved upon the edge of the pool, wanting. Mr. Hoare was a near contemporary of that famous figure, Capability Brown, the romantic exponent of artificial informality. Brown was born at Cambo on the Wallington estate and is reputed to have laid out the grounds there as his earliest work. They are not typical of his style which is

---

[1] Sir Henry Hoare, the present owner, has publicly announced his intention to leave Stourhead to the Trust by will.

best seen at Blenheim, at Croome in Worcestershire or even Clumber. By now the country gentry were taking silviculture really seriously in that they were planting for posterity.

By the third quarter of the eighteenth century the squirearchy was torn between the landscape style rivalries. The Brown, or romantic school, which advocated clumps of trees, winding streams and broad lakes, was bitterly opposed by the pure naturalist or picturesque school, lead by the amateurs Payne Knight and Sir Uvedale Price, who favoured rather the wild, the savage and the gloomy. The bitterness engendered was ludicrous, and Thomas Love Peacock in his satirical novel *Headlong Hall*, points out how each party overlooked the hard and fast conventions that were common to both and palpably obvious to the outsider. Brown's professional successor and champion was Repton who in his day was no less successful. He came from Norfolk and was actually buried at Aylsham, 2 miles from Blickling, where he undertook his last work just before his death. Repton published several essays on the landscapist's art and his famous Red Books show how he intended that narrow streams be widened into crescent lakes, like the one at Clumber, how regi‚ ments of trees be reduced to trim clumps and spinneys, and the aristocratic deer was to take the place of the plebeian cow. One of Repton's most successful examples is to be seen at West Wycombe Park. With the eye of an artist painting from an easel Repton ordered the house the focal point from which each flowing Chiltern contour plays a well‚defined part in the general panorama, the church hill and mausoleum being taken into prominent account, the lake with its Temple of Music. Contemporary oil paintings show a sham yacht kept fully rigged above an elaborate cascade where the waters of the lake fall into the river. Dotted about the landscape are temples to the Four Winds, Daphne, Flora and the other pagan goddesses whom Sir Francis Dashwood loved and at whose shrines he worshipped.

With the nineteenth century, landscape gardening declined into the restricted sphere of the dank and aimless shrubbery. The wide lawns were distracted by fussy little beds until William Robinson came upon the scene and swept them all away. Once more, however, with the popularity of the hothouse, flowers blossomed into their own again.

The importance of the park as an appendage to a gentleman's seat was appreciated long before Brown and Repton. Before they became ornamental, parks were fulfilling a practical purpose. With the decline of the medieval forests it became necessary for noblemen to preserve enclosures for field sports, and so we see them galloping after deer in palisaded areas as depicted upon the wide frieze of the Stag Parlour at Lyme Hall. Fynes Moryson in the reign of James I writes: "Our progenitors were so delighted with hunting as the Parkes are now grown infinite in number and are thought to contain more fallow deere than all the Christian world beside", and under the term hunting must be included all forms of quarry, fallow and red deer, hares, wild boars, birds, wolves, foxes, coneys, otters, badgers, martins and goats. By the seventeenth century falconry became perhaps the most refined art of hunting.

67 West Wycombe Park, Bucking‐
hamshire: the Temple of Music

68 Coleshill, Berkshire: the
Roof Lantern

69 Coleshill: Gate Piers

70 Gunby Hall, Lincolnshire: the Entrance

71 Packwood House, Warwickshire: the Topiary Garden, representing
the Sermon on the Mount

The varieties and species of hawks were infinite. There were the gerfaulcon and the jerkin, the tiercle-gentle, the lanneret, the bockerel and sakaret, the blood-red Rook of Turkey, the waskite from Virginia. The sportsman's relation with his falcon was most delicate and intimate. He must recognise her times of mewing and just how to lure her, the right length of her leather jesses, the quality of her bewets and silver bells and the size and fit of her hood. If these were not precisely to her liking none of his cajolery would win her confidence. This most heraldic of all sports is now completely in desuetude. Fowling was a favourite form of sport and was indulged in "two manner of ways, either by enchantment, or enticement; by winning and wooing the fowl unto you by pipe, whistle or call; or else by engine, which unawares surpriseth them", i.e. netting, liming with twigs and all manner of springes. No birds escaped these machinations, not even the skylark or the nightingale. Falconry and fowling gave way to shooting largely owing to the introduction of the cumbersome long gun about the middle of the seventeenth century, when gentlemen would stalk wild duck or partridges from behind their horses and shoot them sitting. River angling of course had by the time of Izaak Walton reached a zenith from which it has never declined, so that the old muddy tench and carp of the medieval stew pond were dismissed into oblivion.

By the reign of William and Mary sport was so much the criterion by which a gentleman's merits were assessed that he must observe the strictest rules of the chase and the arbitrary fixation of the close seasons. Sport had now come to have that almost ethical significance which the old-fashioned country gentry still attach to it to-day. "The Gentleman's Recreation" of 1697, after an apostrophe of all manners of hunting as an educative value, finally pontificates thus: "Others inflame the hot spirits of young men with roving ambition, love of war and seeds of anger; but the exercise of hunting neither remits the mind to sloth nor . . . hardens it to inhumanity; but rather inclines men to good acquaintance and generous society." The rules of sport soon set the standards of conduct between gentlemen and it was over sport that Robert Walpole and Turnip Townshend, just as a century later Palmerston and Lord John Russell, would settle the affairs of the nation. A Prime Minister, like Trollope's Duke of Omnium, who dared to prefer the pursuit of decimal coinage to that of foxes and pheasants was despised and ridiculed by his colleagues. Sport played amongst the upper classes a more important part than scholarship and moulded the system of public schools until eclipsed by the games system of the late nineteenth century. Above all, field sports account for the peculiarly patrician system of English government in the eighteenth and early nineteenth centuries.

Field sports never became popular pastimes unless we except fox hunting in the nineteenth century. The peasantry, however, from the earliest times had their own rural amusements in which the gentry[1] frequently joined, such as wrestling, bull-baiting and cock-fighting, archery, leaping and vaulting. Of all recreations the one in which both upper and lower classes joined in mutual enjoyment and which served best to unite them was cricket. The first recorded

[1] One childish pastime indulged in by Sir Francis Throckmorton (1640-80), of Coughton, was the whipping top.

cricket match took place at Knole in 1734 between Kent and Sussex in which
Lord John Sackville and Lord Middlesex played for Kent.   The game became
a tradition in the Sackville family and towards the end of the century we learn
much about the prowess of the 3rd Duke of Dorset at this pastime from a
number of ballads celebrating subsequent cricket matches at Knole:

> His Grace the Duke of Dorset came
> The next enrolled in skilful fame.
> Equalled by few he plays with glee,
> Nor peevish seeks for victory,
> And far unlike the modern way
> Of blocking every ball at play
> He firmly stands with bat upright
> And strikes with his athletic might.

With the single exception of cricket the gentry confined their recreations to
field sports that evolved a kind of religious creed in country house circles,
culminating in that New Testament of Sport, the Badminton Library, which
was published in the 1880's.

Religion and politics are delicate factors that simply cannot be ignored in a
study of country house life and manners.   The Reformation indeed launched
country house life, as we know it, and gave great impetus to country house
building.   But for the Reformation, that perjured peculator, Sir William
Sharington, would never have reared his great family mansion round the conventual establishment at Lacock.   On the whole the country gentry of the
ensuing centuries were the products of a triumphant Protestantism, although
in some instances, as at Coughton Court, the Catholic Throckmortons were
able to retain their pre-Reformation association with the property, as were the
Massingberd family with Gunby.   We must none the less face it, domestic life
was riven by religious differences down to 1700 and beyond.   Until this time we
fancy the Protestant Sackvilles, for example, would never have countenanced
intercourse with the Catholic Throckmortons.   From 1700 onwards domestic
life was riven by Whig and Tory differences.   No doubt, by now, the Whig
Hobarts of Blickling would have severely frowned upon social relationship with,
say, the Tory Phelipses of Montacute in spite of the fact that the great grand-
fathers of both families had founded dynasties and built their respective mansions
upon the same ideological foundation, and had certainly shared a common
religious antagonism towards Papists, "those diabolical enemies to God and
Man"—to quote the actual words of the first Phelips.   The first Sir Henry
Hobart was Lord Chief Justice of England under James I, Sir Edward Phelips
Master of the Rolls under the faded Virgin Queen.   These eminent men belonged
to that flourishing profession—and traffic—the Law.   Long after their day the
profession was profoundly suspect and many a rascally lawyer through devious
means started a county family.   Sir John Reresby in his memoirs goes out of his
way to record that his own father-in-law was "ever reputed a very honest
lawyer, which is not very usual".

The Reformation and the get-rich-quick motive induced younger sons of old families to enter trade, a change that came about however but slowly. In 1617 Fynes Moryson writes, "The gentlemen disdaine traffic, thinking it to abase gentry", and one hundred years later Addison makes Will Wimble represent "the case of many a younger brother of a great family who had rather their children starve like gentlemen than thrive in a trade or profession that is beneath their quality." After 1630 many younger sons of Puritan stock, like poor Tom Verney, were sent to America as settlers—and for this purpose there were special agents—or else to volunteer on board a king's ship.

In the sixteenth and seventeenth centuries country house life was little affected by court life. When Mrs. Hutchinson wrote that by the beginning of the Civil Wars "the generality of the gentry of the land soon learned the court fashion and every great house in the country became a sty of uncleanness", she meant that the greater part of the country gentry adhered to the court party and political principles opposed to her own, were Cavaliers rather than Roundheads. The majority of the lesser squires at any rate rarely if ever visited London. They stayed at home and, in between hunting, for the most part ran their estates conscientiously, rode to Assizes and sat on the bench as J.P.s. It is true they were still feudal-minded but the majority of them were beneficent rulers. Servants to them were still servants. At Hatchlands are lists of servants' forfeits—3d. for "indecent language when the cloth is on the table" and for "wiping knives on the table cloth at any time". At Coleshill Miss Fiennes after praising the bedrooms speaks unashamedly of the "chimneys convenient for a servant". The tenantry treated the squirearchy with the distant respect paid to royalty to-day. "Nobody presumes to stir till Sir Roger is gone out of the church", Addison tells us, just as "nobody" would dream of dissenting from the dictum taught in the village school:

> God bless the squire and his relations,
> And keep us in our proper stations.

According to their lights and those of their employees the squires were mostly just and generous men who provided their tenantry with lavish entertainment at the Hall for days on end over Christmastide. As for their wives they brought dozens of children, dead or alive, into the world and attended to the duties of their still rooms "preserving, conserving, candying, making syrups, jellies, beautifying washes, pomatum essences and other such secrets", one of which is Lady Betty Germaine's special recipe for pot-pourri, still to this day used at Knole. What with chivvying servants and providing for large households—and at Knole in Elizabeth's reign there were seldom less than 200 human stomachs to feed—the lord's or squire's lady was fully occupied, with little leisure for dalliance with the blackamoor or for sport with her toy spaniel in the long gallery. In great houses the blackamoor boy, a present perhaps from the younger son now making good in the Barbados, almost invariably appears at the end of the servant's list. His fate is just as invariably the same, a rapid consumptive decline or premature death from an imposthume in his head. In the eighteenth century his place was taken by the Chinese boy, like Hwang-a-Tung whose portrait by Reynolds hangs at Knole. An exaggerated fondness for toy dogs "of the gentle kind" was no less prevalent then than now and Moryson complains scathingly of fashionable mothers who "delight more in their dogs that are deprived of all possibility of reason than they do in their children that are capable of wisdom and judgment".

Since the days of Bloody Mary's Spanish friends foreigners wondered at the prodigality of the English gentry. This was chiefly reflected in their dress at whose extravagance and exaggerated fashions in late Elizabethan times William Harrison with shame records that they laughed immoderately. He himself deprecates "the costliness and the curiosity, the excess and the vanity, the pomp and the bravery, the change and the variety" of their rich materials and the exotic shades—goose-turd green, peas-porridge tawny, popinjay blue, lusty-gallant, devil-in-the-head—of doublet, trunk and hose or of women's galli-gascons and farthingales. A generation later Moryson says the English were far more sumptuous in their attire than the French, and discarded costumes for new fashions before the old were properly worn out. He comments on the profusion of fine jewellery worn by the men, in the length of pearl necklaces worn by the women, and at the same time deplores the uncleanliness of their persons. Lady Anne Clifford in her prolific diary kept at Knole records how during a visit to James I at Tibbalds, "we were all lousy by sitting in the chamber of Sir Thomas Erskine", which is hardly surprising in that upon her own admission she washed her feet and legs at intervals of two months only.

Another indication of well-being in Elizabethan and early Stuart times was the excellence of the food in country houses. According to Moryson, "The art of cookery is much esteemed in England. . . . The English cookes . . . are most commended for roasted meates." Elizabeth personally had encouraged the cultivation of vegetables of all kinds, and loved to risk even "dangerous fruits" from the fields and hedgerows like mushrooms and blackberries. Potatoes came into general consumption in the mid-seventeenth century. Towards the end of the seventeenth century however the quality of English cooking declined into that comfortable indifference from which it has never arisen. English tables, wrote Count Magalotti in 1669, "though distin-guished by abundance are deficient in quality", nor did the upper class English-man's habit, after a meal, of cleaning his teeth with his napkin into a finger-bowl appeal to the fastidious Italian. Since there were only two meals in the day, dinner at eleven and supper at five, vast quantities were consumed at rich tables, what was left over being sent down from the hall to the serving men to finish, over and above their ordinary provisions. They in turn passed over what remained to the poor at the gate. It is not surprising that the English upper classes habitually overeat, indeed, according to Mr. Harold Nicolson, down to the reign of King Edward VII; but until the Restoration they drank but moderately of home brewed ales or heady country wines into which they poured sugar, now a delicacy, previously a medicine only. The wealthy ate off silver, sometimes gold dishes, and drank out of silver, until it was discarded in favour of glass. "Our gentility, as loathing those metals, because of their plenty do now choose rather the Venice glasses." These great meals were usually partaken in solemn silence.

72   West Wycombe Park, Buckinghamshire: the Entrance Portico,
by Nicholas Revett

73 West Wycombe Park: the Saloon

74 Hatchlands, East Clandon, Surrey: the drawing-room, by Robert Adam

If the Elizabethans and Jacobeans were sparing with their wine, a change came with the Merrie Monarch. Drunkenness thereafter was common in high circles. In 1686 at an Alderman's Banquet in London the Lord Chancellor and Lord Treasurer stripped off everything but their shirts and attempted to climb a signpost whereon to drink the King's health. After the Treaty of Methuen the two to three port bottle men habitually ended dinner under the table.

With all the deep spiritual and political convictions of our ancestors, their elegant and luxurious living, there ran a contrasting gay amorality, a toughness and simplicity of conduct that are undeniably attractive. Most grown up men were still intensely superstitious. The Duke of Monmouth on his arrest was found to be carrying in his pockets charms and spells calcu- lated to open prison doors. It was no uncommon thing for masters as well as servants after dark to spy from pedimented lattices black horses without legs drawing chariots to the front door, the occupants carrying their heads under their arms. That misleading abstract, a sense of honour, caused a respectable gentleman like Sir John Reresby, who suffered cruelly for his religious convic- tions in the Civil Wars, to challenge indiscriminately his friends to duel upon the slightest provocation. The Duke of Buckingham ran his sword through Lord Shrewsbury, whose wife was holding the Duke's horse, before carrying her off to an adulterous menage at Cliveden. One of Lord Shrewsbury's seconds in this famous duel was his cousin, Sir John Talbot of Lacock. Sir John was seriously wounded but recovered. His only son, Sharington Talbot, brought the male line of the Talbots of Lacock to an end in another duel, which Evelyn recalls on July 8th, 1685 in his diary. "Came the news of Mon- mouth's utter defeat . . . the batail ended, some words, first in jest, then in passion passed between Sherrington Talbot (a worthy gent^n., Son to S^r. John Talbot, and who had behav'd himselfe very handsomely) and one Captain Love, both commanders of the Militia, as to whose souldiers fought best, both drawing their swords, and passing at one another. Sherrington was wounded to death on the spot, to the great regret of them who knew him. He was Sir John's only son." The sixth Earl of Dorset of Knole who patronized the arts and befriended the indigent was known as "the terror of the city watch", whom it was his recreation to beat unmercifully at nights for the sheer fun of the thing. A nobleman of probity would, if his friend had fallen into political disgrace, hasten to anticipate a sentence of forfeiture by importuning the King for his estates. Marriage was quite shamelessly a market. No delicacy was expressed for the bride and bridegroom's feelings but rather for the fathers' disagreeable necessity of having to haggle like tradesmen over the bride's portion. This for the sake of their gentlemanly honour was often done by proxy. Thus in Charles II's reign Lord Halifax employed a third party to stipulate his term of £15,000 dowry for his son from the daughter of the Duke of Newcastle, who as well as being his brother-in-law and oldest friend, was his nearest neighbour in Nottinghamshire.

The same Duke of Newcastle would travel in winter from Welbeck to London with three coaches and forty attendants on horseback, but the coaches were in effect heavy wagons without springs and with flapping leather curtains instead of glass windows. Lord Winchester indeed took with him four coaches and a hundred horsemen. He would sup at 6 or 7 p.m. over a meal that often lasted till 7 or 8 next morning. "Sometimes he drank; sometimes he heard his music; sometimes discoursed; sometimes took tobacco. Meanwhile the company might do as they pleased, go or come, sit or sleep." At dawn their host might hunt or hawk by torchlight. If it were not fine he might dance. He would go to bed at 11 and sleep till evening. But then Bishop Burnet called Lord Winchester "the riddle of the age". In her cavalcades Lady Anne Clifford even eclipsed these two noblemen for she would turn up unexpectedly at Knole with a retinue of 300. The mileage covered by our ancestors was immense. George III would drive the whole Royal Family from Windsor to Weymouth in one day.

Illness was a dreaded matter and patients never looked to relief from pain. Charles II in his last extremities was made to undergo bleeding, cupping and vomiting. Death was followed by an orgy of mourning, it being respectable for heads of families to lend black furniture and black draperied beds to widowed relations. George III was the first madman whose disease was not treated as a crime. Childbirths and smallpox are cited in all family letters. Colonel Hutchinson in 1638 chivalrously married his Lucy "as soon as she was able to quit the chamber, when the priest and all that saw her were affrighted to look at her", because of her disfigurements. Rich and poor alike pitched their faith upon quack medicines, whose remedial properties lay only in the extravagant names of their ingredients. Lady Anne Clifford treated her child's convulsions with "a salt powder to put in her beer". As late as 1758 Mrs. Delany writes to a friend, "Does Mary cough in the night? two or three snails boiled in her barley water . . . might be of great service to her", while a typical seventeenth century prescription was "snail water, the hiera picra, the mithridates, orbiculi, Bezoartis"!

The eighteenth century undoubtedly witnessed the zenith of country house culture which hardly declined in the nineteenth. At Knole the princely sixth Earl of Dorset entertained Dryden, Montague, Prior, Waller and Pope, "and the best comedy of Dryden's mortal enemy, Shadwell", Macaulay tells us, "was written at Dorset's country seat". A later, ducal Sackville brought Reynolds and Gainsborough there to paint the glamorous Madame Bacelli, who either sat or danced before their canvasses. At West Wycombe Park, Benjamin Franklin and John Wilkes were the frequent guests of Sir Francis Dashwood. Frederick, Prince of Wales, rented Cliveden where Thomson's Masque of Alfred was first performed and Dr. Arne's strains of "Rule Britannia!" were first chanted. Gladstone, Garibaldi and Queen Victoria were visitors of a later era. At Wallington, Swinburne, Millais, Ruskin and William Bell Scott pursued pre-Raphaelite principles. At Lacock Abbey, Mr. Fox Talbot invented photography. And in fact, down to the outbreak of the war the great houses of England still served as a background for the pursuit of the arts, sport and politics, and only a few years ago the so-called Cliveden House Party set was the familiar designation of a group of Members of Parliament, to which Mr. Winston Churchill belonged.

75 Dinton Park, Wiltshire, by Sir Jeffrey Wyatville

77 Mrs. Jordan, by Thomas Phillips, at the Court,
Holt, Wiltshire

76 Bennet Langton, by Sir Joshua Reynolds, at Gunby
Hall, Lincolnshire

If this chapter provides a glimpse into the past of a fraction of our historic country houses, how are we to envisage their future in the brave new world ahead of us? Few apparently will remain private family residences for long. In the meantime the National Trust has endeavoured to effect a compromise in the case of those houses where the donors' families still reside. For the most part they now reside in a part only of the building, the rest being treated as show rooms, or if in the whole house the chief rooms are open to the public at stated times. To-day there is much speculation about adult education colleges, rest centres and public institutions of all kinds using these houses. Such a solution the Trust welcomes and encourages in spite of the multifarious complications involved. For it must be borne in mind that the Trust's primary responsibility is to preserve the fabric of the historic houses under its guardianship, their gardens and grounds, their rich interior decorations and their valuable contents, and above all their character, unimpaired.

VII

COUNTRY BUILDINGS

By BASIL OLIVER, F.S.A., F.R.I.B.A.

ENGLISH people, especially those living abroad and those whose lot it is to work in urban surroundings, are justifiably apt to become nostalgic by thoughts of their beloved native countryside. But above all it is the unique character and charm of the typical English village forming part of the landscape which most engenders these emotions.

The reason for this deep-rooted affection is not far to seek, though it is not always realized that it arises primarily from the invariable use, by our fore-fathers, of local materials for all kinds of buildings, be they church, manor house, inns or cottages, so that they look, and are, indigenous and blend naturally with the scenery.

One need only recall the severely simple stone-walled and slate-roofed cottages and farm-houses of the fells and lake districts; the whitewashed cob and thatch of Devon; the stone-built gabled houses with mullioned windows of the Cotswolds; or the timber-framed buildings of Cheshire, Herefordshire, Worcestershire, East Anglia and the South-Eastern Counties where timber was plentiful and stone, in the cases of Norfolk, Suffolk and Essex, almost non-existent as a building material.

For the latter reason brick has never been used to better purpose than it was in the Eastern counties in Tudor times and later: the use of flint in Norfolk and Suffolk has survived continuously from prehistoric times.

No building could better express the ruggedness of Cornwall than the fourteenth-century stone-built Old Post Office in Trevena village, Tintagel, near Boscastle, which was bought by the National Trust for £200 in 1903.

Could fitness for purpose be more appropriately expressed than in the tile-hung and weather-boarded cottages of Kent, Sussex and Surrey? Such external protection was essential in those counties, and no modern inventions have excelled in efficiency such a satisfactory combination of practical advantage and totally unselfconscious beauty. Tile-hanging on old buildings is excep-tional north of these three south-eastern counties wherein weather-boarding is also found more generally than in other parts of England.

"Weather tiles were hung", writes Mr. Curtis Green, R.A.,[1] "on oak laths and were bedded solid in lime and hair mortar" and "were fastened with pins of hazel or willow, and sometimes of elder. . . ."

In the Eastern Counties, especially in Essex, since the fifteenth century, or even earlier, weather-boarding was largely used for wind and water-mills, frequently for barns and other farm-buildings, occasionally for bell-turrets of churches and sometimes for the exposed weather sides of houses, just as slate-hanging was used in Lakeland and Cornwall.

[1] *Old Cottages and Farmhouses in Surrey,* pp. 26 and 27.

78 West Wycombe Village, Buckinghamshire

79 Lacock Village, Wiltshire

80   Chiddingstone, Kent

81   The Court House, Long Crendon, Buckinghamshire

White paint is the most usual protective covering and certainly looks better than tar which is much favoured in districts where the weather is exceptionally severe. In Norfolk it is commonly found in association with roofs covered with red or black-glazed pantiles, more especially on farm buildings.

The all-over plastering put, in the seventeenth century, on timber-framed structures of the two preceding centuries was done purely for greater comfort within, yet it is now the unwise fashion to strip off these protective coverings. East Anglian ornamental pargetting arose from making "a virtue of necessity".

Of minor examples of the country architecture of England—with a few in Wales—the Trust, at the present time, owns the villages of West Wycombe, Buckinghamshire; and Lacock, Wiltshire; also the small group of ten thatched cottages, designed by Nash, collectively known as Blaise Hamlet, Gloucestershire; Broadclyst, Devonshire, on the Killerton Estate; Selworthy, Allerford, Bossington and Luccombe, included with the Holnicote Estate; part of the village of Montacute, Somerset (included with Mr. E. E. Cook's gift of the mansion, both through the Society for the Protection of Ancient Buildings); and individual buildings of greater distinction in the same two counties; three dissimilar but thoroughly indigenous properties in Kent; two East Anglian cottages; cottages in Berkshire, Hampshire, Wiltshire, Oxfordshire and Surrey; numerous scattered Lakeland farmhouses and cottages, etc., in Cumberland, Lancashire and Westmorland; cottages in other distant counties, i.e. Northumberland, Carmarthen and Cornwall; clergy houses in Sussex and Somerset; court houses in the Lake District part of Lancashire, and in Buckinghamshire; water-mills in Essex, Cheshire, Norfolk, Worcestershire, Huntingdonshire and Surrey; one windmill only, and that in Buckinghamshire; bridges in Yorkshire, Westmorland and Surrey; dovecotes in Bedfordshire and Somerset; and, amongst a number of barns, one especially good example in the latter county.

This summary, listing and classifying the Trust's properties according to the order of their strength and approximate importance, is deliberately given to show, almost at a glance, how widespread and diverse they are; which counties of England and Wales are so far represented; and which are not. In the order given above so they will be referred to.

Conspicuously absent from the list are typical examples of the very individualistic stone buildings of the Cotswolds though it is right to mention that Arlington Row and other important parts of the delightful village of Bibury, Gloucestershire (William Morris's favourite village), have been transferred to the safe keeping of the Gloucestershire Archaeological Trust, via the Royal Society of Arts.

It has to be admitted that there are still some lovely villages still in danger of thoughtless disfigurement and even downright vandalism, unless some kind of tactful control is exercised.

It is good indeed that two such typical villages as West Wycombe and Lacock, as well as parts of other villages, have come under the protective care of the Trust, but there is still scope for some such further safeguarding, more particularly owing to the shortcomings of Ancient Monuments legislation. The

Act, notwithstanding amendments, still precludes the scheduling of inhabited buildings which is not only a weakness but is often a danger.

Not all villages are alive to their national value and some are surprisingly careless of their local show-place value, but one that is the former and not the latter is the famous Suffolk village of Lavenham where influential inhabitants have co-operated with their own local authority (i.e. the Cosford Rural District Council), to form a new body called the Lavenham Preservation Society, with the Society for the Protection of Ancient Buildings as their chosen advisers.

This is a wholly admirable development as far as it goes, and is particularly opportune before the big programme of necessary and inevitable post-war housing schemes everywhere materialize.

It has been rightly said that ". . . local authorities ought to be encouraged to take a pride in their inheritance . . ."[1] which is precisely what the Lavenham authority intends to do.   Their action should serve as an example for those charged with the care of other beautiful villages.

One would feel easier in mind if villages like Kersey, Suffolk; Finching-field, Essex; Ombersley, Worcestershire; or Groombridge, Kent (and others named elsewhere in these pages) would take steps to protect themselves as Lavenham has done.

With regard to individual buildings worthy of preservation an examination of the Trust's county classification of properties best reveals where representation is strong, weak or non-existent.   In course of time it is to be hoped that the second category will be strengthened and the third remedied.

It may here be well to name the counties wherein there is room for improvement so far as minor vernacular architecture is concerned.

In Bedfordshire the Trust's only building of architectural merit is a dovecote; in Glamorganshire, Herefordshire and Nottinghamshire the Trust's holdings do not include any building; and in the counties of Brecknockshire, Cardigan-shire, Leicestershire, Montgomeryshire, the Soke of Peterborough, Radnorshire and Rutland it has, as yet, no property of any kind.

Perhaps the most conspicuous gap is Herefordshire and it is not a little surprising that no example of a typical widely-spaced timber-framed Hereford-shire building such as are still extant in Pembridge, for instance, has yet come to the Trust.

It is true that the cottages of Worcestershire and Warwickshire are similar but the Trust has no old cottage property in any of these three counties.   The acquisition of a village—or part of a village—in any one of them, before it is too late, seems to be worthy of consideration.

The more closely-spaced half-timber work of East Anglia (e.g. the Guildhall, Lavenham, Suffolk), is almost unrepresented amongst the Trust's possessions, neither has it any example of East Anglian seventeenth-century pargetting apart from the restored Sun Inn at Saffron Walden; nor has it many characteristic Norfolk brick houses (apart from Blickling Hall and a few seventeenth-century farmhouses on the estate), preferably one showing Dutch influence, reed-thatching, and the use of flints for walling.   Suffolk also has any number

[1] Mr. E. H. Keeling, M.C., M.P., House of Commons, 11th July, 1944.

of good brick houses of the sixteenth, seventeenth and eighteenth centuries, yet none is owned by the Trust.

If vernacular architecture is to be fully represented it should also include a few good tile-hung and weather-boarded examples.

The solid and simple stone-built cottages of Yorkshire and Derbyshire are other notable absentees, examples of which would make the list more comprehensive.

Dorset, Gloucestershire and Wiltshire types also need strengthening; and a good cottage example of Cheshire "magpie" work would not be amiss.

Thus it will be realized that much is lacking.

VILLAGES: WEST WYCOMBE, BUCKINGHAMSHIRE

West Wycombe, Buckinghamshire—2½ miles from High Wycombe on the Oxford road—together with its larger neighbour and the surrounding district, has, for generations, been the centre of the chair-making industry. It has, or had, two factories which provide employment for most of the inhabitants.

The village consists of a pleasantly winding street, containing some fifty dwellings (including two inns), which date from Tudor to Georgian times.

The story of the acquisition of West Wycombe really begins in 1926 with the reading of a paper on *The Preservation of Ancient Cottages* before The Royal Society of Arts, by the late Sir Frank Baines, then Director of Works in H.M. Office of Works (as it was until recently known). This event resulted in the Society calling two conferences, the first in 1927, presided over by the then Prime Minister, Mr. Stanley Baldwin; and the second in 1929 when his successor, Mr. J. Ramsay Macdonald, took the chair. The fact that Prime Ministers presided on both occasions testified to the importance which they at least, as the nation's leaders, attached to the ever-increasing threat to our heritage of cottage architecture.

The outcome of these conferences was an appeal issued by The Royal Society of Arts which led to the collection of approximately £15,000, and the forma-tion of a standing committee to administer the Fund. After various detached properties had been bought from time to time the Society conceived the idea of purchasing, if possible, a whole village so as to focus more effectively public attention and, it was hoped, gain more general support for the Cottage Preserva-tion Fund. This was a bold venture, for the repair of cottage property in an old village, as everyone knows, is no light matter.

Within a week of the Society being informed, in March 1929, that the greater part of the village of West Wycombe was in the market the Council resolved to expend the remainder of the Fund, with subsequent donations, to purchasing the property.

Thenceforward the Committee concentrated on the highly necessary task of reconditioning the cottages whose state in many cases was deplorable owing to more than thirty years of neglect to keep them in repair, due to the fact that there had been no resident landlord on the estate during most of the time.

Under the skilled direction of Mr. William Weir—than whom no architect better knows how to handle old buildings without depriving them of their charm—a wonderful transformation was brought about, this being mostly confined to internal improvements and to the belated introduction of such amenities as piped water supply, proper sanitation, electric lighting, gardens, etc., rather than to changes in external appearances.

When all this had at last been accomplished and almost the whole of the Society's newly-acquired property put in first-rate order, it was, in February, 1934, in its entirety formally handed over to the National Trust for permanent preservation, at a reception given by the Trust at the Goldsmith's Hall.

Great credit is due to the Royal Society of Arts for its initiative and energy in rescuing at least one unspoilt English village, and to the Trust for subse-quently spending £17,000 on reconditioning.

The Trust has continued the good work started by the Society. After it had become the owner of the major part of the village it received, in the follow-ing year, as a gift from Sir John Dashwood, the 59 acres constituting Church Hill, and during the year 1943-44 he has added the still more munificent gift of his beautiful house, West Wycombe Park with 300 acres of grounds.

Even this is not quite the last chapter for in 1943 the Trust inaugurated a competition for the design of a group of workers' cottages to be built on the site of a demolished chair factory. Mr. Edward Maufe, A.R.A. and Mr. Darcy Braddell were the two other architects appointed to act with Mr. William Weir as co-assessors to adjudicate on the designs received, of which there were no less than 257. They placed first that submitted by Messrs. T. Mellor, G. Grenfell Baines and J. A. Ashworth, all three Associates, R.I.B.A.

The carrying out of their joint design will add yet something more to this happy and unique sequence of events which it is a real pleasure to record.

It is hoped that West Wycombe will remain for all time the typical example of an old country village; this it had become by reason of the many kindly changes made there since the fifteenth century, the date perhaps of the earliest buildings now standing.

VILLAGES: LACOCK, near CHIPPENHAM, WILTSHIRE

With her gift to the Trust, during the year 1943-44, of Lacock Abbey Miss Matilda Talbot included the village of Lacock and Manor Farm, the deeds of all of which she presented to Lord Esher on behalf of the Trust on November 4, 1944. Lacock Village,[1] to the south-east of Chippenham, shares with Castle Combe, to the north-west of that town, the reputation of being one of the two most famous show villages in Wiltshire; it is much to be hoped that Castle Combe may eventually also be similarly safeguarded.

The unspoilt beauty and splendid preservation of Lacock village is chiefly attributable to several centuries of happy relationship between successive generations of good squires and their contented tenants. Historical and architectural data concerning Lacock Abbey (the "big house" to the villagers), are given on another page and they help to account for the general atmosphere of the background which had made the village what it is and prevented it

[1] "Lacock . . . has been selected by the British Council for the making of a photographic record of the life of an English village." *The Times*, Thursday, September 14, 1944.

82　Cottages at Selworthy, Somerset

83, 84 Blaise Hamlet, Gloucestershire, by John Nash: from a contemporary aquatint

from becoming what it might have developed into but for such fortunate continuity. There are not more than 400 inhabitants all told but many of the families, the Selmans, the Selfs, the Taylers and the Hunts are said to have dwelt in Lacock since the Abbey was built in 1229. It has ever been the invariable practice of the Trust to bring, and keep, its farms and cottages up to modern standards of equipment and convenience so that the inhabitants of Lacock, as indeed all the tenants on the estate, have nothing to fear from the recent change of ownership which so closely affects them.

VILLAGES: BLAISE HAMLET, an adjunct to BLAISE CASTLE, GLOUCESTERSHIRE

Blaise Hamlet or Henbury Cottages, at Blaise, near Bristol, Gloucestershire consists of a group of ten small gabled cottages, some of them thatched, irregularly placed about a green. In one respect they are unlike other buildings of their kind in that they were deliberately designed to be picturesque—perhaps a trifle selfconsciously so—and did not just happen like the great majority of old English cottages.

Their chief interest lies in the fact that their designer was none other than John Nash, the Regency architect whose formal classical stuccoed architecture of Carlton House Terrace, Regent's Park, and the original—but destroyed— Regent Street has brought him great fame.

"This group", writes Mr. John Summerson, "is in the nature of an anthology for many of the cottages reproduce designs carried out seven or eight years earlier on other estates. One reproduces the keeper's lodge at Sarsden, Oxfordshire; another is identical with a cottage at High Legh; another with a cottage at Hilton, for Mr. Vernon. The varied ingenuity of the combination of hips, gables, verandahs, and porches is very engaging; taken as a whole, the group is perhaps the worthiest memorial of Nash as a cottage romanticist. . . ."[1]

In 1809 the then squire[2] of Blaise Castle,[3] conceived the idea of erecting homes for old retainers of his family. With all the right instincts of a good land-owner and country gentleman it is obvious that appropriateness and pleasant appearance dominated his mind when instructing his architect, but to Nash belongs the credit for so planning his layout that a woman standing in her doorway should not be able to see any of the other nine doors, his, or his client's quaint idea being to prevent, or at least to minimize, village gossip.[4]

The tall pump, surmounted by a sundial, on the green covers a spring that never fails in the driest summers; its happy design incidentally affords further evidence of Nash's enjoyment of his playful interlude.

This early and almost unique example of architect-designed cottages of the period was purchased during 1943-44, largely with the help of the Gryphon trustees, Mr. Donald Hughes, the vendor, and other friends.

[1] *John Nash*, by John Summerson, p. 100.
[2] John Scandrett Harford, banker, who died in January, 1815.
[3] "Castle" conjures up visions of a Norman stronghold but it is here in fact the name misleadingly applied to a stone country house, of scholarly classical design, built in 1795 and typical of its period and purpose.
[4] *Country Life*, March 31st, 1900, Vol. VII, No. 169.

VILLAGES and COTTAGES on the KILLERTON ESTATE, DEVON; on the HOLNICOTE ESTATE, SOMERSET; and in MONTACUTE VILLAGE, SOMERSET

Two of the six outstanding acquisitions of the year 1942/43 were the Killerton Estate, Devonshire and the Holnicote Estate, Somersetshire.

The former includes Broadclyst—a pleasantly typical Devon village without, however, any particularly noteworthy buildings—situated about 7 miles north-east of Exeter.

The latter estate is on the northern edge of Exmoor, near Minehead, and includes the widely known and beautiful villages of Selworthy, Allerford, Bossington and Luccombe.

These estates together form the largest single acquisition of the Trust and were acquired from Sir Richard Acland, Bart., M.P.

The Holnicote Estate runs down to the sea north of Porlock. The view given of Selworthy—of picture postcard fame—with the slopes of Dunkery Beacon in the background, well exemplifies the traditional Somerset arrange-ment of externally projecting main chimney diminishing in size from ground-level upwards, approximately central on the front of the house, usually next to the entrance doorway. Originally this was the only chimney but each of the Selworthy cottages in the photograph selected, has a second chimney at one end of the building which may have been added at some later time. Semi-circular bread/ovens were built projecting from the base of the chimney, at its widest part, an example of which can just be detected in the more distant cottage in the illustration.

At the foot of the great rolling heather-covered hills in Porlock Vale—immortalized by Southey's poem—lies the pretty little hamlet of Bossington, most remembered for its fine old walnut trees, the trunk of the largest having a girth of approximately 15 feet, with some of its branches as much as 40 feet long, both of which records are perhaps explained by the great age of the tree, reputed to be over 500 years old.

The National Trust is particularly rich in architectural possessions in Somerset, even apart from the vast acreage covered by the Holnicote Estate and these are of interesting and varied character.

When, in 1931, Mr. E. E. Cook, with great generosity, made it possible for the Society for the Protection of Ancient Buildings to purchase the magnificent stone mansion at Montacute—4 miles from Yeovil on the Ilminster road—the property included 24 cottages in the village and 303½ acres, the whole of which was subsequently transferred to the Trust. The gradual repair and improvement of the cottages and farmhouses has been in progress ever since. All were in a poor state and the sanitation was out of date and inadequate.

For example, Bay Tree Farm, adjoining The Gables—a pleasant cottage which has been rethatched—had a flat/pitched slate lean/to roof over the back quarters, under which were two low damp bedrooms, quite unfit for human habitation. The back wall has been raised in the form of two gables and a new roof has been made beneath which are now two good bedrooms and a bathroom with proper sanitation.

By 1935 the cottages had all been made fit for habitation although some further improvements remain to be carried out. Notable among the smaller houses is one at the Borough entrance to the gardens. This late fifteenth- or early sixteenth-century house has been repaired and a little added to and is now a comfortable house.

THREE KENT PROPERTIES

By far the most pleasing examples of the minor domestic architecture of Kent, belonging to the Trust, are the timber-framed houses and cottages, including the Castle Inn, at Chiddingstone—8 miles south of Sevenoaks and 4 miles east of Edenbridge. These form a delightful group.

It was in 1939 that the Trust purchased the greater part of the village out of funds provided by the Fallowes Bequest together with restrictive covenants over 6 acres of adjacent land.

Loose Wool House, in the village of Loose—3 miles south of Maidstone— is a fifteenth-century house, of a similar form of timber construction, which was formerly used for the cleaning of wool. It was left to the Trust in 1934 by the late Colonel J. C. B. Statham with some furniture. In addition to its own original grounds part of a field opposite the house was acquired in 1935, making 1½ acres in all, and the property was further protected in the same year by restrictive covenants over a piece of land at the back of Fairview Cottages. This old house has since been repaired and converted into two houses, now both occupied.

Tudor Yeoman's House, at Sole Street, Cobham, is a typical and authentic hall-house of Kent, well named to suggest its age and purpose. The usual Elizabethan in-built chimney and oak beams carrying the inserted bedrooms in the upper part of the hall have been removed. Obtained and restored by Sir Herbert Baker, K.C.I.E., R.A., who gave it to the Trust in 1931.

TWO EAST ANGLIAN COTTAGES

A characteristically East Anglian building, in beautiful surroundings, is Willy Lott's Cottage on the Suffolk bank of the Stour at Flatford, a name made famous by John Constable, the great English landscape painter. This is a charming little sixteenth-century timber-framed house, externally plastered and lime-washed; with steep-pitched roofs, at three different levels, covered with dark red weathered hand-made sand-faced local tiles.

No better example of unstudied arrangement of gabled roofs could well be found.

This is one of the group of three buildings more fully referred to in the *Shrines* section. These properties, together extending to 16 acres, came to the Trust during the year 1943-44 after they had been put into proper order, though when, in 1925, Willy Lott's Cottage first came before the Committee of the Society for the Protection of Ancient Buildings—with whom the Trust works in such close and happy accord—it was in a very dilapidated condition. Part of the roof was off and the half-timber walls had reached that state of decay when they could only remain standing for a few years. A scheme put forward for the founding of a School of Landscape Painting at Flatford Mill, when, it was suggested, this house might become the home of one of the instructors, unfortunately came to nothing.

The Trust has since acquired this interesting group of properties from the executors of the late Mr. T. R. Parkington, of Ipswich. Only recently this group of buildings has been leased to the Council for the Promotion of Field Studies.

In the same part of England, though in a different county, is a small thatched house, formerly two cottages but now converted into one, and known as Berg Cottage (to perpetuate the memory of its donor), at Barkway, Hertford-shire—4 miles north of Buntingford and the same distance south of Royston.

This little building, with the date 1687 over its porch, stands in the village street opposite the Almshouses; it had become sadly derelict and dilapidated and would have been condemned by the local authority but for the timely intervention of the late Miss M. Berg who bought and presented the property in 1938 after careful reconditioning by Mr. William Weir.

The timberwork of the interior is typical of the best cottage workmanship in Hertfordshire, Essex, Suffolk and East Anglia generally; it is in fact of much the same type as Willy Lott's Cottage referred to above.

The "before", "during" and "after" photographic records of this interesting transformation are some of the most revealing in the Trust's possession. If these could be widely exhibited they might well be the means of saving, from needless demolition, other such border-line cases.

COTTAGES, etc., in BERKSHIRE, HAMPSHIRE, WILTSHIRE and OXFORDSHIRE

Priory Cottages, Steventon, Berkshire—4 miles south of Abingdon on the Newbury road—consist of five cottages forming three sides of a small open court including part of a block of timber-framed buildings originally built as a monastery.

They are situated at the end of a long line of similar buildings facing a delightful old causeway raised about 3 feet above the ground with a cobbled track bordered with a fine avenue of trees on top of the bank.

The roof over the cottage at the back of the courtyard is of special interest. This portion of the building was originally a single storey hall with a magnificent hammer-beam truss in the centre, the single moulded upright of which comes down between the two windows on the external wall of the ground floor and the other in the corresponding portion against the court. Mr. John E. M. Macgregor in his Report, dated February 6th, 1936, suggests that the construc-tion generally points to the roof having been ". . . originally formed with a tie-beam and converted later to the hammer-beam form of construction, the change probably taking place shortly after the original construction. . . ."

One timber-framed cottage is evidently of Jacobean date and certainly of the character of that period, with its two-storeyed bay and drop-finials to the soffit of the overhanging gable above. Good as it is now it will be still more attractive when it has been reconditioned. Another cottage also timber-framed, but in this case thatched, is also good of its kind, though sadly dilapidated at the present time. The whole group was presented in 1939 by Ferguson's Gang. As soon as possible after the war is over these quite exceptional cottages will be made habitable.

This will be a satisfactory beginning, but the quantity and quality of the fine old buildings in this famous Berkshire village are such that nothing less than complete acquisition by the National Trust—as in the cases of West Wycombe, Buckinghamshire and Lacock, Wiltshire—would permanently safeguard its beauty.

In the neighbouring county of Hampshire two thatched cottages and an inn were presented in 1929 by Sir Buckston Browne in memory of his wife. These are Vaine Cottages and Woodman Inn, Sparsholt—3 miles west of Winchester.

In another adjacent county, namely Wiltshire, the Trust now owns, apart from Little Clarendon, the cottage-home of William Lawes, the composer, at Dinton, near Salisbury. This is a stone-built house with stone-mullioned windows and thatched roof, all very characteristic of the county though perhaps the sentimental interest here predominates over the architectural.

The Trust is poorly off for properties of any kind in Oxfordshire, possessing three in all, only two of which are buildings.

These are Coombe End Farm, a seventeenth-century house $1\frac{1}{2}$ miles north of Pangbourne in the parishes of Goring and Whitchurch.

This farm comprises 194 acres of agricultural land at the southern end of the Chilterns, held to preserve the amenities of the district.

Presented in 1932 in memory of her husband, Sir Rickman J. Godlee, by Lady Godlee who remains in occupation for her lifetime; and two cottages, built probably in the middle of the same century, known as Little Bartletts, South Leigh, $2\frac{1}{2}$ miles east of Witney, presented by Miss Jacobs in 1937.

SURREY COTTAGES

Godalming, Surrey. Eashing Cottages.

These three ancient cottages—two of typical Surrey widely-spaced timber construction and one of brick—form a valuable group with Eashing Bridges,[1] also owned by the Trust. The attention of the Society for the Protection of Ancient Buildings was first drawn to the bad condition of the cottages by one of its members in 1922, and this resulted in the Committee asking for an opinion upon them by a local correspondent, who, finding that the owner was unwilling to have the necessary repairs done, enquired if he would sell them. This he agreed to do at a reasonable price. The sum required was raised by the West Surrey Society who contributed over £100, and by a contribution from the National Trust, who also promised to put them in repair and to hold them for the nation.

The work was entrusted to Mr. John E. M. Macgregor—one of the Society's architects who has since become its technical adviser. Reconditioning and internal modernization were at last put in hand in 1939 but necessarily proceeded slowly because of the difficulties of war conditions, and the job was not completed until November, 1941. It was decided to convert the two small timber-framed cottages into one, with living-room, sitting-room, bedroom, kitchen, etc., on ground floor; with two bedrooms and combined bathroom-W.C. upstairs. He has contrived the same accommodation in the brick-built cottage though in this case the third bedroom is on the upper floor. Thus the fortunate tenants have the advantage of modern living standards of comfort within an externally beautiful building. This is a satisfactory result of the Society's action.

In Surrey also the Trust owns other cottage property in Godalming itself, known as Ockford Road Cottages. These are on the west side of the main street at the south end of the town, and were presented in 1925 by Mr. H. Avray Tipping as examples of how old cottages can be suitably repaired for modern conditions.

LAKELAND FARMHOUSES and COTTAGES, etc.,
in CUMBERLAND, LANCASHIRE and WESTMORLAND

Thanks to the popularity of *Peter Rabbit* and to the generosity and public spirit of its authoress, Beatrix Potter (Mrs. William Heelis), the Trust during 1943-44 acquired under her will the many properties she owned in the Lake District.

During her lifetime Beatrix Potter did much to preserve the beauties of her own neighbourhood by gifts to the Trust, by herself buying threatened areas, and by her practical example as a farmer and breeder of Herdwick sheep.

This new bequest includes Penny Hill sheep-farm, adjoining the Trust's holding in Eskdale, the farmhouse being a typical Cumberland building containing some old furniture of the local type; also farms, woods and cottages at Coniston, Skelwith, Little Langdale—where the scenery is especially charming—Hawkshead and Sawrey, all in Lancashire; and Troutbeck sheep farm at the head of the Troutbeck Valley.

It is hoped that at some future date—and in collaboration with Mr. Heelis—Hill Top Farmhouse, where Beatrix Potter lived and wrote many of her books, will be arranged as a permanent memorial to her, and some of the original water-colours which illustrated her books preserved and exhibited there. More recently Castle Cottage was her home.

As well as Hill Top Farm practically the whole of the village of Near Sawrey belonged to Mrs. Heelis; and besides the properties already mentioned on the

Lancashire side of Little Langdale she owned two farms on the Westmorland side, i.e. Busk and Dale End. These are typical small sheep farms with white-washed houses and grey buildings; and the land is particularly beautiful.

These properties constitute the greatest gift the National Trust has ever received in Lakeland and increase the area of land already owned from about 14,500 acres to over 18,400 acres. The will also provides for a sum of £5,000 to be put in trust for improving or adding to the new acquisition.

Quite apart from this Beatrix Potter bequest other possessions of the Trust in the Lake District include Seathwaite Farm, Borrowdale, Cumberland; Thwaite Farm and Hawkshead Court House,[1] both in Lancashire.

The Trust also owns Bridge House, Westmorland, in Ambleside on the Rydal Road. This is an unusual building on a small bridge over the Stock Ghyll, the two together forming a striking whole, probably dating from about the end of the seventeenth century. The superstructure is now used as a shop though it may originally have been a garden house or look-out. It was bought by local subscriptions in 1928.

The severely simple long low farmhouses and cottages of Lakeland, with their whitewashed stone walls and Westmorland grey-green slated roofs, all look much alike and seem to call for neither further description nor comment; their greatest virtue being the wonderful way in which they blend and harmonize with the landscape and seem to add to it a kind of human touch which serves to enhance its interest without ever marring its beauty. Would that one could say the same of modern buildings, often with most unsuitable roofing materials, now so indiscriminately dumped on the countryside without a thought given to their disastrous effect upon it.

COTTAGES in other distant counties:
NORTHUMBERLAND, CARMARTHEN, CORNWALL

Amongst the 900 or more cottages owned by the Trust in more distant counties are those in the village of Cambo, Northumberland, which forms part of the Wallington Estate (in which Sir Charles Trevelyan, Bart. retains a life interest); those comprising most of Pumpsaint village on the Dolaucothi Estate, Carmarthen, given by Mr. H. T. C. Lloyd-Johnes (subject to his life interest), as a permanent memorial to the Johnes family; and lastly three cottages known as Wayside Cottages, St. Agnes, Cornwall, presented by the Misses A. M. and H. M. Bulkley, subject to their life interest and that of a third sister. None of these, however, is of any particular individual merit, but Cambo is an interesting example of eighteenth-century village layout.

Though the St. Agnes cottages are less picturesque than the Old Post Office, Tintagel, they are none the less characteristic Cornish buildings of local stone and roofed with scanteles, their chief value being that they are the only ones of the kind now remaining at St. Agnes.

[1] Included elsewhere under *Court Houses*.

CLERGY HOUSES, etc.

Authentic Clergy or Priests' Houses are rare but the Trust is fortunate in possessing two examples, both of the fourteenth century, and each characteristic of the architecture of its county and period. These are Alfriston Clergy House, Sussex—timberframed and thatched—and Muchelney Priests' House, Somerset—stonebuilt and also thatched.

These were the residences of the parochial or secular clergy of preReformation times, and were the houses in which the priests serving a parish lived together, having one common hall or diningroom and smaller apartments for individual use. In both cases it was the vicar of the parish who recognized the historic value of these interesting survivals and took the first steps towards reinstating and preserving them for the nation.

The Old Clergy House at Alfriston—in the locality of Eastbourne, 4 miles northeast of Seaford, between Alfriston Church and the Cuckmere River—was bought in 1896 in a very ruinous condition and repaired out of funds specially subscribed. After application, with the consent of the then vicar the Rev. F. W. Beynon, had been made to the Lord Chancellor—as patron of the living—to the Bishop of the Diocese; and to the Ecclesiastical Commissioners, for the transfer of the building, ". . . with reasonable means of access thereto on all sides . . ." the property was eventually made over to the National Trust for the nominal sum of £10, and was subsequently reconditioned with the cooperation of the Society for the Protection of Ancient Buildings.

Apart from its historic and architectural interest it also marks an important milestone—actually the first of its kind—in the annals of the Trust, for in the Report from March, 1896 to July, 1896, financial assistance is sought in the following words: "It is to be hoped that the supporters of the Trust will not allow its first purchase to be rendered abortive through lack of funds to carry out the necessary work of maintenance. . . ."

The building had been altered almost beyond recognition through conversion into labourers' cottages, but it had been unfortunately allowed to fall into a state of great dilapidation, as is only too clearly shown by photographs in possession of the Trust, taken at the time of its acquisition.

The oak framing is exceptionally and beautifully massive, the interstices being filled in with "wattle and daub" in the usual manner of the period, and at least two centuries later. The central hall is open to the roof which has large cambered tiebeams and moulded kingposts.

Muchelney Priests' House—1½ miles south of Langport—is a typical and wellpreserved example of a small fourteenthcentury building, with windows apparently of the two succeeding centuries inserted, though the form of the entrance doorway indicates that it is part of the original structure. This charming little building was bought in 1911 by public subscription and repaired under the supervision of the S.P.A.B. and is now occupied by a tenant. Before its acquisition it had been used as the Glebe House and, owing to the care with which it had been preserved in its original form, is an almost unique building of its class.

It is arranged on the usual plan, with opposite doors, hall, solar, etc. It has a wide entrance passage, with north and south entrance doors with moulded pointed arches. On one side of the passage there is a living room, with two bedrooms over used as a labourer's cottage, when Mr. Thackeray Turner included a note on the house in the S.P.A.B. Annual Report of 1908. On the opposite side there was then a schoolroom and sitting-room, used as store-rooms. The house is surrounded by a walled garden.

In 1908 the building was in urgent need of repair; and, as a result of correspondence with the vicar, he was furnished with a report. By 1911 the excellent incumbent being alive to its worth and to the need for its preservation, offered the house and garden to the National Trust for £200.

NOTE—Another of the Trust's Somerset possessions is Bruton Dovecote, referred to on page 95.

Another property, originally devoted to ecclesiastical purposes, as its name implies, is Church House, Widecombe-in-the-Moor, Devon—6 miles north of Ashburton and 11 miles from Newton Abbot. Part of it is used as a cottage, while the rest, which has been repaired, is now the village hall. This rather unattractive granite building, with its long, straight, hard-looking roof, somehow gives little indication of its age which is said to be of the fifteenth century. It has a comparatively modern continuous verandah in front of the ground floor, above whose roof are small mullioned windows with rounded heads to the lights, the central feature of the façade being formed by a taller mullioned and transomed window, the upper part of which breaks through the eaves in the form of a small gablet.

COURT HOUSES

The Trust is the owner of two Court Houses in widely different counties; one, built of stone, in the Lakeland part of Lancashire; the other, of timber-framed construction, in Buckinghamshire.

The Lancashire example is Hawkshead Court House, situated at the junction of the Ambleside and Coniston roads, half a mile north of Hawkshead. This is a pre-Reformation building, of ecclesiastical appearance, with low-pitched stone-slate roof, with stepped gables and small high two-light stone-mullioned windows in the main front wall, immediately under the eaves; it is entered by a central rough low porched arch. Higher up in one of the gabled ends is a larger two-light window with traceried head, apparently of the fifteenth century. This small picturesque building was presented to the Trust in 1932 by Mr. H. S. Cowper, F.S.A., under whose direction it had been repaired. The Court Room is used by the Boy Scouts.

Long Crendon Court House, Buckinghamshire—2 miles north of Thame and 14 miles from Oxford—is a fourteenth-century Court House or Staple Hall close to the Church. This is a timber-framed structure, with brick fillings between the widely-spaced uprights. It has a partly overhanging upper storey, but with long continuous eaves giving the appearance of a braced recess at one end. The upper room, containing some fine beams and trusses, is used as a child welfare centre, while the ground floor serves for cottages. This interesting building, which is a good example of its kind, was bought for a nominal sum from Lady Kinloss, All Souls' College and the Ecclesiastical Commissioners in 1900 and repaired out of special donations.

MILLS

Bourne Pond Mill, Colchester, Essex—1 mile south of the centre of the town —is a striking little building with gables in the Dutch manner, erected on the site of a medieval mill, or monk's fishing-box, in the last decade of the sixteenth century, out of older materials from St. John's Abbey, whose last abbot was hanged in 1539, for disputing Henry VIII's supremacy over the Church. The Abbey gallows were at Bourne.

This building was presented with the garden and mill-pond of 4 acres by an anonymous friend in 1936 with the benefits of a restrictive covenant over $2\frac{1}{2}$ acres on the east side of the mill.

A further half-acre by the pond was protected in 1938.

It is said to have been a cloth mill before it became a corn-mill; though long since disused for either of those purposes it was still grinding meal down to May, 1935, when part of the machinery gave out.

The presence of a tall graceful octagonal stone chimney, as the central feature of each end gable, may however indicate that the present structure was originally built for a different use such as possibly a fishing temple—as its precursor may have been—or as a dwelling-house. However this may be it is the Trust's intention to undertake repairs so that the building can be used again, in some form or other, as soon as post-war conditions permit, under the architectural supervision of Mr. Marshall Sisson.

The form of the two fireplaces, which have yet to be opened up, one at each end of the building, in its upper part, rather supports the domestic theory. Both have Tudor heads contemporary with, and similar to, that of the main front entrance.

This mill is of a quite unique type, and for that reason its value is the greater; it also has an interesting history, for it was built, as the inscription[1] in its south end testifies, in 1591, by Sir Thomas Lucas, who had been Sheriff of Essex in 1568 and Recorder of Colchester about the year 1575. His arms, quartering two other coats, are over the entrance.

Fortunately it remained undamaged after the Siege of Colchester in 1648 when Sir Charles Lucas (the Royalist grandson of its founder), and Sir George Lisle, Colchester's two famous heroes, lost their lives after bravely defending the town.

The walls are composed of a colourful jumble of flint, bricks (of varying length and thickness), tiles and stones, with "galleting" or "garetting", as the insertion of small chips of flint into the wide mortar-joints is known: and with stone quoins, door and window-dressings, string-courses, etc.

The form of the gables with their elaborate finials—eight to each, a few of

---

[1] "Thomas Lucas Miles, Anno Domini, 1591."

85 The Priest's House, Muchelney, Somerset

86 The Clergy House, Alfriston, Sussex

87   Bourne Pond Mill, Colchester, Essex

88   The Tudor Dovecote at Willington, Bedfordshire

which are damaged, is so characteristic of the Low Countries that this picturesque example, as Mr. J. Alfred Gotch has pointed out ". . . could hardly
have been anywhere but in the Eastern Counties. . . ."

The National Trust's wise policy is that its architectural possessions shall
not remain merely interesting museum pieces but shall, whenever possible, be
put to some useful purpose such as this building will be when, in due course,
it is given a new lease of life as a most desirable residence in its self-contained
oasis of peaceful calm in the suburbs of Colchester.

The largest of the Trust's mills is Quarry Bank Cotton Mill, a good plain
Georgian building erected in 1784 and the oldest cotton mill still working,
presented in 1939 by Mr. A. C. Greg, together with the village of Styal—
1½ miles north of Wilmslow, Cheshire—built shortly after the mill itself. Mr.
Greg included with these gifts 250 acres covering a long stretch of the Bollin
Valley from Twinnie's Bridge to the Boundary of Oversley, some fine woodlands, and an interesting half-timbered farmhouse—in all a happy combination
of natural beauty with architectural interest.

Next in size and importance is Burnham Overy Mill, Norfolk—1 mile
north of Burnham Market on the road from Hunstanton to Wells—a three-
storeyed structure forming part of a group of red brick buildings round the
mill-stream, of which the others are the Maltings, the Mill House (*circa* 1820)
and three cottages, with 39 acres of arable and marsh land. Purchased in
1939 with funds from the Fallows Bequest and the Hon. Alexandrina
Peckover.

One of the Wyre Forest properties is Knowles Mill, Worcestershire—
1½ miles north-west of Bewdley—this is a stone and brick building, in an
attractive setting, with 4 acres of orchard in the Dowles Valley, presented by
Mr. Paul Cadbury in 1938.

Houghton Mill, near St. Ives, Huntingdonshire, is a picturesque example
of a weather-boarded water-mill given to the Trust in 1939 by the River Ouse
Catchment Board, and endowed by Lieutenant-Colonel Tebbut. It has
now been adapted to serve as a Youth Hostel to which good purpose it is
likely to revert as soon as hostilities have ceased, as in the case of the Trust's
Mill at Winchester.

Another of the same kind is Shalford Mill, Surrey—1½ miles south of Guildford opposite the Sea Horse Inn at Shalford. This is an eighteenth-century
timber-framed building with projecting tile-hung gable, supported by front
corner-posts, forming a kind of lofty verandah, or covered way, below, to the
water's edge; on the Tillingbourne with a small garden. Repaired, endowed
and presented in 1932 by Ferguson's Gang.

Ivinghoe Windmill, Buckinghamshire, between Ivinghoe and Pitstone—
3 miles north of Tring, and 3½ miles from Cheddington—is the only windmill
owned by the Trust and was acquired in 1937. This is a post-mill standing
alone in the middle of a large field. It was long derelict, but has now been put
in good repair though its missing sails have not been renewed and it has long
ceased to be a working mill. Apart from being an interesting—though
mutilated—survival it is now merely a prominent landmark and serves, alas,

no other purpose. According to the late Mr. Donald Smith[1] ". . . The round-house of yellow brick was a comparatively recent addition. . . . The trestle timbers have some good moulding, but had apparently weathered a good deal before the addition of the round-house. It carries the dates 1637 and 1749, and is stated to have ceased working in about 1894. It has now no ladder, tail-post or sails. There are remnants of the machinery still in position and two large millstones on the top floor. . . ."

NOTE—Flatford Mill and Mill House, near East Bergholt, Suffolk, is referred to in the *Shrines* section.

BRIDGES

Stainforth Bridge, Yorkshire—2½ miles north of Settle on the old packhorse route from York to Lancaster, is a beautiful single stone bridge over the Ribble, at least 200 years old, the curve of its graceful arch being particularly satisfying.

Before it was acquired in 1931, the Trust consulted the S.P.A.B. as to this bridge's architectural value, and the financial responsibility attaching to it, and a technical report answering these questions was duly made.

". . . The Bridge is a typical example of stone arch work of that district and, being founded on rock, may be considered permanent. It is exceptional only in the fact that the span is greater than all others in the neighbourhood and also because of its picturesque setting. Further, since it crosses a poorly metalled by-way only, and is not part of direct communication between any largely populated areas, the bridge will not be altered for the sake of increasing traffic facilities . . ."[2]

The acceptance of this bridge by the National Trust assures its preservation.

A smaller stone bridge over Stock Ghyll, Westmorland, also belonging to the Trust, is that with a small house upon it to which reference has already been made with the Lakeland properties.

Charming Surrey examples are the Eashing Bridges—1½ miles from Godalming and close to the Guildford by-pass road.

These two bridges, over the Wey, are said to date from the time of King John. They were presented with their approaches and a sum for their main-tenance by the Old Guildford Society in 1901. They are of similar design to other interesting medieval stone bridges on the upper reaches of the river Wey at Elstead, Tilford (E), Tilford (N), and Unsted. All are built of narrow stone slabs and, except in the case of Unsted bridge, have the peculiarity in common that their cut-waters on the down-stream side are semicircular; they also have wood or iron rails instead of stone parapets.

Another half-acre near the right bank of the river was presented in 1931 by Sir Emery Walker in memory of his wife, further to safeguard the approaches; and it seems appropriate here to mention that three old cottages[3] opposite the bridges were presented in 1922 by Mr. Thackeray Turner and the West Surrey Society.

[1] *English Windmills*, by Donald Smith, Vol. 2, p. 129. Published in 1932 by The Architectural Press.
[2] From a note written by the late A. R. Powys, C.B.E., F.S.A., Secretary of the Society for the Protection of Ancient Buildings, in the Society's Annual Report, 1932.
[3] Particulars of these are given on page 87.

89   The Old Post Office, Tintagel, Cornwall

90   Eashing Bridge, Surrey

91   The Market Hall, Chipping Campden, Gloucestershire

92   Paycockes, Coggeshall, Essex

DOVECOTES

The Trust owns a number of dovecotes of which two are outstanding. The earlier and more imposing is at Willington, Bedfordshire—4 miles east of Bedford—a dovecote of Henry VIII's time, of considerable architectural interest, purchased in 1914 with an acre of land. This is a stone-built structure, with a two-tiered tiled roof having stepped gables at each end. The building is divided into two parts, approximately equal, with the dividing wall carried up above the roof, also stepped like the end walls. Each part is separately entered in front by a low Tudor doorway which, more than any other feature, affords the best evidence of its period.

The other dovecote is at Bruton, Somerset—5 miles north of Wincanton and ½ mile from Bruton across the railway. Though this building is smaller than the Willington dovecote it also is of sixteenth-century date and built of stone, with all four sides gabled and of exceptional height.

It was presented in 1915 by Sir Henry Hoare and subsequently repaired by the Society for the Protection of Ancient Buildings, before being finally taken over by the Trust in 1922.

When the Society was first consulted, in 1914, about this well-known local landmark its condition was such that it was in danger of falling. Although the estimated cost of minimum repairs to keep the building standing was no more than £200 subscriptions were slow in coming in because of prevailing war conditions, but nevertheless the appeal eventually succeeded. Local feeling was strong that in view of the difficulty in obtaining labour and materials it would be wiser to postpone the work; as the bulk of the Repair Fund had been collected in the district, the Committee could only acquiesce. Consequently it was not until 1922 that the work of repair could be carried out, under the auspices of the Society, and the building taken over by the National Trust.

Unfortunately sufficient funds were not available to roof the building in, but the walls were repaired and strengthened, and the interior repointed where it was necessary to prevent the wet from entering.

BARNS

Amongst the Trust's barns one of more than usual interest is West Pennard Court Barn—3 miles east of Glastonbury and 7 miles south of Wells, between West Pennard and Baltonsbury, which adds still further variety to the many Somersetshire properties.

It was repaired and presented by the Society for the Protection of Ancient Buildings in 1938 chiefly through the generosity of Mr. Roger Clark, of Street, a member of the Society.

This is a fifteenth-century barn, beautifully conceived on simple symmetrical lines, in five bays, with a roof of particularly interesting construction. It stands practically in the centre of a half-acre field about half a mile south of the village of West Pennard, and was built with all the refinement and high finish that one is accustomed to find in the great tithe barns of such monasteries as Glastonbury and Abbotsbury; yet it is a small building (measuring internally 60 feet by 24 feet), perfectly adapted to the needs of the village. It is also unusual in that it originally had a dovecote at the east end, the roosting holes being formed in the east end of the barn, but this building has now been replaced by a shed.

The barn was in a deplorable state when Mr. John E. M. Macgregor, Technical Adviser to the S.P.A.B., inspected it on September 10th, 1932. It was still in the same state—with nearly half its roof gone and with one end and part of adjacent roof smothered with ivy—in February, 1936, the date of the photograph which appears in the Society's Annual Report for that year.

The Report for the following year, however, shows the barn on the completion of its particularly skilful repair, under the direction of Mr. Ernest E. Bowden, with its original form restored, its beauty enhanced and again fit for its proper purpose.

The tenant, at the time of Mr. Macgregor's visit, had already gone so far as to obtain an estimate for removing the remains of the old roof, lowering the walls and erecting a flat-pitched corrugated iron roof!

So this catastrophe has been averted, and the barn's rehabilitation is, in every respect, a matter for congratulation. The building has been given a new lease of life and will stand for years as an exemplar of competent repair.

VIII

TOWN BUILDINGS

By JOHN SUMMERSON, F.S.A., A.R.I.B.A.

A TOWN is two things. First, a community; second, a fabric. The fabric ought to fit the community, but never does; some of it is always out of date. Perhaps in periods of busy peacefulness the buildings in a town may very nearly catch up with what the people want. I imagine that Lavenham in the first half of the sixteenth century was very nearly a perfect fit, right down to the ornaments and inscriptions on the houses, all new enough to be understood and cherished at their precise social and symbolic value. I dare say the same is now true of Letchworth.

But in times of sweeping change the community outgrows the city. The process is unconscious, silent and sinister, since nobody sees what is happening till it has happened. The fiction of the old community survives, crystallized in habit and in the old landmarks; and the new community grows into a queer shape, because it lives, as it were, in a house too small for it, and has to stick its head out of the roof when it dines, and its legs out of the windows when it goes to bed, which is not only uncomfortable and unwholesome for the community, but destructive of the house.

This sort of thing has been happening all over England. Look at Coventry, which I always think of as the most stark and "diagrammatic" example I know of the collision of different ways of life, and different kinds of architecture. Before the war, one would meet the bedesmen of Bablake Hospital going to church in Tudor gowns. Many streets were still largely sixteenth and seven‑ teenth century, built for men who made and sold woollen caps to the world outside their Gothic walls or fed or armed the makers and sellers of woollen caps. All this fitted the spired skyline and the medieval picture. But going farther down the street one came to the Coventry of the ribbon‑weavers and watchmakers—dirty red streets of grim little three‑storey houses with long workroom windows under the eaves. There were, and still are, miles and miles of this Coventry, quite intact, the legacy of industries which have been stone dead these eighty years. Farther still, one came to the houses built in living memory, built for the cycle trade, the small‑arms trade, the sewing‑ machine trade. But still the real present‑day Coventry was elusive until one realized that it was writhing—a huge invisible entity—through the whole city; until one looked again at Hertford Street and Cross Cheap and found that nearly every shop belonged to a chain store; until one realized that the cappers' houses and the ribbon‑weavers' houses were teeming with factory‑hands from Triumph, Singer, Rudge and Armstrong‑Siddeley, and until one realized, too, that Coventry's boundaries now stretch out past Stoke and Edgwick, Earlsdon and Whoberley; and that the three spires wield their dominion over nearly a million souls. When the spires were built there were perhaps 20,000.

Something like this, though on a less enormous scale, is happening in nearly every town in Britain. The old fabric is being stretched and torn and shattered because a new community is trying to use it. And it doesn't fit.

Now, in this rather ugly scene which is going on in every direction, the National Trust is, I take it, concerned with one thing; to acquire and protect, wherever it sees the opportunity, those parts of the old fabric of our towns which have some value apart from their use as living-space, and which can play a part, even if it is a purely aesthetic part, in the life of the community *as it actually is.* To do this successfully involves two issues. First, the determination of a policy as to what is worth keeping in a changing town. Second, a shrewd notion as to how the kept buildings can be used. Some years ago, in a paper on preservation which I read to the Architectural Association, I formulated five categories of buildings which I thought ought to be considered as either certainly or possibly worth preservation. I here indulge my second thoughts and revise the wording of the categories, and although I do not claim the quintet as "watertight", I do not think it leaks very badly. Here are the five:

1. The building which is a work of art: the product of a distinct and out-standing creative mind.
2. The building which is not a distinct creation in this sense but possesses in a pronounced form the characteristic virtues of the school of design which produced it.
3. The building which, of no great artistic merit, is either of significant antiquity or a composition of fragmentary beauties welded together in the course of time.
4. The building which has been the scene of great events or the labours of great men.
5. The building whose only virtue is that in an otherwise bleak tract of modernity it strikes an effective and romantic contrast.

Obviously, several quite different basic kinds of values are involved in all these cases. They could be grouped under two heads—aesthetic and literary. Literary values (by which I mean those associated with history and a sense of continuity), are never absent from an old building. Aesthetic values very often are. Aesthetic values are rarer, more precious and more closely integrated with a structure than literary values, and I have therefore put those buildings which embody them at the head of my list of worthy objects of preservation.

Now, accepting the validity of my five categories, it will be interesting to apply them to the list of twenty-one urban properties held by the National Trust. It ought to enable us to discover some relationship between values and opportunities, and to answer the question—what sort of a building does public opinion think worth preserving? For I take it that in most of these cases acquisition by the Trust has been preceded by some degree of local or national discussion, interest and feeling.

94   The George Inn, Southwark

93   The Great Window in the King's Head Inn, Aylesbury

96 A Chimneypiece in the Treasurer's House

95 The Treasurer's House, York

The first thing that strikes me about the list is that hardly any of the buildings qualify for my first category. Few of them are, in any special sense, "works of art". The Assembly Rooms at Bath provide the outstanding exception, for here is a building which in plan, in the organization of its parts and in the detail, bears the stamp of a cultured and original mind. I would not say that John Wood was a very great artist, but he certainly was distinguished by more than ordinary ability. If the Bath Assembly Rooms had no historic association whatever, their preservation would still be worth considering. As it is, of course, the building could qualify triumphantly under Category 2, and a good case could be made out under Category 4.

An important thing to remember about buildings which are clearly "works of art" is this. Their value depends on form, not on sentiment. Therefore, if they are damaged or destroyed, their value under Category 1 is undiminished, provided they are accurately reconstructed in new materials. I understand that the Assembly Rooms are to be rebuilt, and this is perfectly right and proper. The fact that the new ornaments and sash-bars will not be precisely those upon which Beau Nash set eyes does not matter in the least. They had collected no "patina" of age, and relied on no irrecoverable sense of craftsmanship for the pleasure they gave. Personally, I find great enhancement in reconstructed classical architecture. I like the new, sharp-cut masonry of Peckwater quad-rangle at Christ Church, and wish that much more of Oxford's scrofulous architecture could be "touched for the King's evil" in the same effective way.

To come back to the list. I doubt if any other building really qualifies for Category 1. I am sorry about this, because I think the first obligation on conservators is to protect buildings which crystallize high flights of imagination and high levels of technique. On the other hand, I admit that there are com-paratively few such buildings in our towns, and that the Trust possesses country houses which in this respect are superlative. But the kind of building I mean is the house or villa which in quality of design is miles above the ordinary run of similar buildings in its locality. In London, I would mention as an example, No. 7 Adam Street, the one intact portion of the old Adelphi. Villas at Clapton, Wimbledon, Richmond and Greenwich occur to me. At Reading there is an exquisite house by Soane in one of the main streets (it is now a vicarage and therefore, I presume, fairly safe); at Norwich there is a house by Robert Mylne (now a tea-shop and apparently in good hands); at Nottingham there are three or four little masterpieces of the 1780's by an architect whose identity I do not know. These are the sort of buildings which *must* be secured for posterity, but which, being small private houses, not prodigiously old and very simple and subtle in design are *caviare* to the general (which sometimes includes, I am afraid, the mayor and corporation), and are likely to be swept away without anyone being any the wiser, but with the nation's treasure that much poorer.

In my second category, which comprises buildings possessed of routine virtues in a pronounced form, I can place several items from the Trust's list. There is the Treasurer's House, York, with its early seventeenth-century façade, wrought-iron gates, and wealth of remarkable interior detail, everything good of its kind; there is Bank House, Wisbech, which has all the excellent qualities of not too pedantic Palladianism; there is No. 3, Cheyne Walk, obviously the work of a typically competent London craftsman of the same period; there is Quebec House, Westerham, another eighteenth-century house of good solid quality. All these are valuable acquisitions, and Quebec House qualifies again under Category 4, from having been the residence of General Wolfe.

But it looks as if Category 3 is the one in which most of the Trust's acquisitions qualify most easily. Undoubtedly public opinion favours antiquity before anything else as a certificate for protection. Indeed, all of us feel kindly disposed to a building which has managed to come through to us from the Middle Ages. For the Middle Ages are inaccessibly remote from ourselves and a medieval building is, in effect, a message from a lost world; however meagre its artistic claims it is difficult to make a case for removing it. The vast bulk of our medieval heritage is in the hands of the church, but here and there are alienated or secular structures which have taken their chance in the rebuilding market and arrived after many hazards at the twentieth century. Several such buildings now belong to the Trust. There is Aberconwy, at Conway, a medieval fragment now appropriately used as a museum. There is Westbury College, near Bristol, with its interesting gateway and the priests' houses; the college has association with Wyclif and Canynge and therefore qualifies twice. There is Buckingham Chantry Chapel, rebuilt in 1474, but retaining a Norman doorway; and there are the Tudor merchant's house at Tenby and Paycockes at Coggeshall. These last two are very important relics of medieval domestic life. The Tenby example is one of the few houses of its kind surviving in Wales. And Paycockes is, of course, one of the finest medieval houses to be found anywhere. Not only that. Its history is well documented by the Paycocke wills, as everybody knows who has read Eileen Power's essay on the Paycocke family in *Medieval People*.

I qualified my terms of inclusion for Category 3 with the word *significant*. By *significant* antiquity I mean antiquity which has more than its own, intrinsic, sentimental value. Paycockes, because of its attractively human documentation, is significant in this sense. Another building where significant antiquity is beyond dispute is the George Inn, Southwark. Here is the living survivor and representative of all those galleried inns which, from medieval times, were massed along the southern approach to London. It is a small and not specially beautiful building, but it tells a tremendous story touching every generation of Englishmen from Chaucer's to Sam Weller's. One would have to travel as far as Gloucester to find a comparable example of this kind of building; and the National Trust rightly perpetuates this miracle of a survival in Central London.

Also in Category 3 must be placed Joiner's Hall, Salisbury, and the Sun Inn, Saffron Walden, both good examples of ancient houses; together with Little Fleece, Painswick, St. John's Institute at Hackney, with its fine panelled rooms, and the King's Head, Aylesbury. Grantham House, an attractive multi-period building, also qualifies here, and so do the market houses at Chipping Campden and Winster. These last two buildings have that con-

97 The Assembly Rooms, Bath, by John Wood, now gutted

98   The Ballroom in the Bath Assembly Rooms

99   The Concert Room in the Bath Assembly Rooms: from the aquatint
by J. C. Nattes

spicuously architectural character which belongs to buildings raised on arches and standing on open sites; and the Campden example is such an interesting composition that I am not sure that it ought not to go in Category 1.

And now for buildings "which have been the scene of great events or the labours of great men". I regard this category with grave suspicion, perhaps for the following reason. For years I entertained a great regard for a house in which, as I understood, my grandfather had lived; later, I was told that he had never set foot in the place. Of course, I was disappointed, and quite lost interest in the house, until I was grown-up enough to realize that it was a pleasant, late Georgian cottage anyway, when I evaluated it accordingly. But the point is that the house served its high romantic purpose to admiration so long as I was deceived into believing that it had been my grandfather's. In other words, the objective fact that a certain man did live in a certain house is of purely subjective value. Why, the great man *himself* may never have been conscious of the house where he lived, apart from the fact that the creeper on its wall bloomed once a year, and that the rate-collector called once a quarter.

I am always rather distressed by the preservation of Keats's house in Hampstead. He was singularly unhappy there, and, although it is not a bad thing to recollect and understand the unhappiness of a long dead poet, the mummification of the *milieu* where it all happened seems to me horrible. I would be sorry if Keats's house was pulled down, because it is a pretty house with a large, pretty garden which one can see from the road. But there is a very much better house nearly opposite, which I would much rather endow with permanence, even if, as I imagine, nobody more important than some obese Georgian nabob ever lived in it.

The National Trust owns, among others, the London house inhabited by Carlyle, and Wordsworth's house at Cockermouth, both pleasant houses in a small way. Neither Carlyle nor Wordsworth, however, evinced any particular sympathy for architecture (though Carlyle did once deign to observe that Chelsea Hospital appeared to be the work of a gentleman), and it seems to me that, in principle, this line of preservation is very dubious, and very difficult to conduct satisfactorily.

From this generally suspect principle, however, I must make distinct exception in the case of houses which have been the architectural creature of their owners—I mean houses like Strawberry Hill and Abbotsford, in which the owner's taste and scholarship are structurally incarnate. Sir Joseph Banks's house in Soho Square was such a case; its demolition, in the 1930's, was a disaster. There was a house which accurately reflected the personality and habits of a very remarkable man. Its façade to Soho Square had outstanding merits of its own, and the interior included the elegantly ceiled square hall which Sir Joseph had specially built for his scientific meetings. Dozens of famous men must have known that house, which was, in fact, one of the cradles of modern science and discovery. I have an ugly feeling that if it could have been shown that Charles Dickens had a dream about little Nell in the second floor back, that house might have been saved.

Of the last of my five categories I need say nothing, because the intrinsically

15

unimportant things which I intend it to include are rather small game for the National Trust. And yet, I wonder. The Trust owns such architectural *bagatelles* as the cottages at Squires Mount, and how infinitely poorer Hampstead Heath would be without them!

And now, looking back over the list of the Trust's urban properties, what does it show? It certainly shows a rich and charming variety of architecture. It shows perhaps that buildings of antiquity and archaeological value find their way most readily into the Trust's hands; but it also shows, in principle, a lively catholicity. One significant omission occurs to me. Although the Trust possesses several groups of houses (e.g. Squire's Mount, which comprises a number of contiguous properties) it possesses no *formal* groups. One of the great problems of architectural conservation is to protect the really good terrace, the crescent and the square. How admirable it would be if the Trust owned such a masterpiece of formal grouping as, say, the Paragon at Blackheath or Pelham Crescent at Hastings, or even (to fly as high as possible) the Royal Crescent at Bath! I write this in utter ignorance of possibilities and probabilities and of established policy in such matters. But it would be grand to see the Trust's holding of urban properties as broadly and boldly on the increase as its holding in the countryside.

It is obvious that our English towns are going to be rebuilt. Not, I suspect, quite as soon or as completely as certain brightly illustrated volumes of plans and perspectives would lead us to believe; but still, probably during the next half century. We shall hardly live to see the new towns, but this generation will be largely responsible for the essential spade-work, both in creation and conservation. It is this generation's responsibility not only to create but to see that certain inherited achievements of intellect and imagination embodied in building materials and in parks and gardens are handed on safely to the future. Now is the critical time, the turning point, when our conservators must have a thousand eyes and must wield the rapier with one hand and the bludgeon with the other, and make their voices heard in council and in the market-places —especially the market-places.

The National Trust has grown to mature age and ripe wisdom, and amply justified the intuition of its founders. Its record as conservator of the countryside is magnificent. In the towns it has done noble work, but there is much more worth doing. The opportunities are great. Let us hope that the wisdom of the Trust and the sense and sentiment of our age will, together, see that they are not lost.

IX

HISTORIC SHRINES

By JOHN RUSSELL

IT is a very proper part of the National Trust's work to take into stewardship not merely those buildings and properties which are in themselves remarkable, but also others whose claim upon our interest is primarily one of association. It is with some of these places that this chapter is concerned. In such matters, everyone lays his own tripwires; and an association or twist of memory which may pull one traveller up sharp may leave another placidly free to continue his way. The Trust cannot take so subjective a view as is displayed in these pages; it necessarily embraces every kind of sympathy, and among its properties are many which might be included in this chapter; every reader could make another list, and ignorance or preoccupation, rather than malice, is responsible for my own omissions. It is in any case a pleasure to think that the Trust has in its care so many places which, from their association with memorable men, are now among the best emblems of our past.

Something (Whistler's grizzled mummy, perhaps) sticks in the way of our imagining a youthful and beardless Carlyle. In point of fact, however, he did not stop shaving until 1854; and when in the spring of 1834 he first came to Cheyne Row he was in appearance a young and vigorous man, arresting by the great breadth and strength of his jaw, and the brooding command of his eye. (Maclise had admirably seized his look at this period.) Cheyne Row is now a tolerably grand street, and not one which a man would choose who (as was Carlyle's case at the time) might not earn a penny from his profession for two years together. Carlyle explains this: "Chelsea is unfashionable", he wrote to his wife, "it was once the resort of the Court and great, however; hence numerous old houses in it, at once cheap and excellent." No. 24 was soon found much superior to its rivals in Brompton and Bayswater. It was well placed; a friend, Leigh Hunt, lived within a gunshot (not that either of these house holders was likely to fire a gun); from the back windows nothing could be seen but the perfection of *rus in urbe*, varied by the "topmost dome" of St. Paul's and the wraith of a City spire. Genteel persons (of the piano owning class, said Leigh Hunt) lived in the neighbouring houses, though from one window one might see "rather dim houses" and even "questionable miscellanea, among other things, clothes drying". A few paces away, where Boehm's statue of Carlyle now stands among municipal evergreens, Carlyle paused on his first visit to admire the river view. The Parade then comprised "shops, etc., a broad highway, with huge shady trees; boats lying moored, and a smell of shipping and tar; Battersea bridge (of wood) a few yards off; the broad River with white trousered, white shirted Cockneys dashing by like arrows in their long canoes of Boats; beyond, the green, beautiful knolls of Surrey with their villages;

on the whole a most artificial, green-painted, yet lively, fresh, almost opera-looking business such as you can fancy".

Mrs. Carlyle took a less rhapsodical view. The interior of the house had been most favourably represented to her. The "massive old concern", she said, could not fail to please, with its dressing-room to every bedroom, possibilities of a shower-bath, and endless room for crockery; but all waterside houses were damp and unwholesome, wainscot was a terrible waster of candles, and might there not even be bugs? These doubts were soon overborne, and on the 10th of June 1834 the Carlyles took possession of No. 24 Cheyne Row, at a rent of £35. They were poor; their kitchen arrangements were for a long time augmented by hampers and presents of wine from attached friends; their furniture also was eked out. In the large double room which runs the length of the ground floor, the drawing-room carpet from Craigenputtock was carefully enlarged with strips of dyed blanket. The best of their pictures from Scotland hung above a bust of Shelley and alongside a print from Dürer, both given by friends. Later there was a steady addition of family baubles; Mrs. Carlyle made a four-fold screen, pasted all over with oddments; a friend celebrated his return from the Crimea by giving the Carlyles a box of steel and cedar-wood; an article on Jean-Paul Richter enabled Carlyle to buy a four-poster of Scotch fir; and by the end the house was quite fashionably full. Carlyle was not a truly companionable man, and he spared his wife none of the tiny props and miseries which can poison domestic life; but once at least he acknowledged her skill. "You are like an Eve", he said, "and make a little Paradise wherever you are." It was, however, a paradise into which he begrudged others entrance. Some could overcome this; Tennyson for instance would call at two o'clock and stay until eleven; but after other visits Carlyle would speak of the intruder with savagery ("a diseased rosebud", for example), or confess that "nobody comes whose talk is half so good to me as silence". Only one formal entertainment seems ever to have been given at No. 24. "The other week", he wrote in March, 1839, "Jane audaciously got up a thing called a soirée—that is to say, a party of persons who have little to do except wander through a room or rooms, and hustle or simper about, all talking to one another as best they can. It seemed to me a most questionable thing. However she was drawn into it insensibly and could not get retreated; so it took effect—between twenty and thirty entirely brilliant bits of personages—and really it all went off in a most successful manner. At midnight I smoked a peaceful pipe, praying it might be long before we saw the like again."

In 1834 Carlyle bought "a large lamp of the sinumbra kind". The speciality of this was that it cast light without shadow; though it was prized by both Carlyles, there could be no more inappropriate symbol of domesticity as it existed in Cheyne Row. Light (though of a fitful, smoky kind) was certainly cast, and over many unfamiliar places; but with what extravagance of shadow, one may sense from Mrs. Carlyle's letters and from despairing passages in her husband's journal. Carlyle, in Froude's words, "wrote always in a highly-wrought quasi-automatic condition, both of mind and nerves". One may indeed imagine by what mental and nervous ferment the history of the

French Revolution and of Frederick the Great came to be set down in Carlyle's rhapsodic and pictorial style—the baronial Gothic, one might say, of English prose. He was in short a difficult man, engaged upon difficult work. It is enthralling at the present time to judge from the great mass of evidence how shrewdly he foresaw the rise of Germany; walking in summer through the cool and shady house one may imagine that in this room, or in that, Carlyle sat and heard the huge machines of force majeure
Tune up for murder.

Germany, he thought, should be President of Europe; Phallus-worshipping France and "torpid, gluttonous, sooty, swollen and squalid England" would be shown their places. These visions served only to plunge him in Cimmerian gloom, however; and below, his wife would struggle to prepare mutton pie and raspberry tart against the arrival of diners. Mealtime seems not to have been an occasion for rejoicing at Cheyne Row; for although intellectually such galaxies can rarely have been seen around a poor man's table, the digestion of both host and hostess was chronically weak. Alsop the chemist was kept busy with orders for blue pills, for Seidlitz powders, for castor oil; but even these often caused only some more radical disaster, tempting both partners to self-slaughter. In vain was the hour of dinner switched through a wide arc of possible times; the biliary condition never mended. Mrs. Carlyle detested walking—the "most toilsome of all sublunar employments"; but Carlyle was always flinging out of the house, prowling up and down the King's Road, or tearing as far as the furze groves of Wandsworth Common or "the sunny precincts of Tooting". Often he was in a state for which his wife's epithet ("ill-haired") seems a kindly diminutive; but sometimes the now vanished poetry of the south bank of the Thames would calm him. One hot evening in August 1840 he walked over Battersea Bridge, and thence "by a wondrous path across cow fields, mud ditches, river embankments, over a wide space of what attempted to pass for country. . . . Boat people sat drinking about the Red House; steamers snorting about the river, each with a lantern at its nose. Bewildered-looking, mysterious coke furnaces (with a very bad smell) glowered at one place. Windmills stood silent. Blackguards, improper females, and miscellanies sauntered, harmless all. Chelsea lights burned many-hued, bright over the water in the distance—under the great sky of silver, under the great still twilight. So I wandered full of thoughts, or of things I could not think." In a miniature way the garden of Cheyne Row gave solace also; he had always liked, in summer, to wander about it in his dressing-gown and straw hat, smoking; gradually they had added to its resources until cherry, lilac and plane trees, a grape vine, hawthorn, jessamine, wallflowers and mint made it almost a pleasaunce. After his wife had died in 1866 the garden, which had still in it her favourite bushes and flowers, became almost a shrine for him; and sometimes (on a clear night in October 1869, for example), it would touch off some deeper intimation—or in his own words, "a strange new kind of feeling", that of his own transience before "God Almighty's own Theatre of Immensity, the INFINITE made palpable and visible". It is thus true to say that the house in Cheyne Row was for forty-six years not only an intellectual bakery of exceptional proportions, but also the real, as much as the geographical, centre of its owner's life.

In the autumn of 1867 Carlyle went with Lord Stratford de Redcliffe to visit Woolsthorpe Manor, near Grantham, the birthplace of Isaac Newton. Carlyle, with that pejorative turn which seems to have been natural with him, had long since demoted Newton ("once my grandest of mortals") from any position of eminence; yet Newton "has always this of supremely notable—that he made the grandest discovery in science which mankind ever has achieved or can again achieve. Wherefore even I could not grudge the little pilgrimage to him". Woolsthorpe was probably some twenty years old when Newton was born in 1642. It is a small and compact limestone manor house in the Cotswold tradition, such as might have been built by any well-to-do gentleman farmer; many of its internal features have been preserved. So also has the apple orchard; a cutting was taken recently from a descendant of its original trees, and it was established that the putative jolt to Newton's giant mind was given, if at all, by a now extinct variety of apple, the "Flower of Kent". One may fancy that though Newton reputedly watched the falling apple from an upper window, yet he must often have paced his garden during intervals of reflection. In middle life, at Cambridge, he was said not to be able to bear the sight of a weed in his garden; and often, after a short turn in the open, he would pelt upstairs to pursue some new train of ideas. Woolsthorpe has a particular fascination for all who honour the great forward leaps of the human mind; for it was there, when driven from Cambridge by the plague in 1665 and 1666, that Newton formulated three great discoveries—the differential calculus, the composition of light, and the law of gravitation. "In the two plague years", he said later, "I was in the prime of my age for invention, and minded mathematics and philosophy more than at any time since." At Cambridge his curiosity, as great as Leonardo's, was diffused over a vast range of subjects; he not only computed the area of the hyperbola to 52 figures, but studied cider-making, the design of ear-trumpets, the prospects for reformed spelling, the preparation of artist's colours and the usefulness of kites. He also found time to dine out, to lose money at cards and to go shopping for oranges. At Woolsthorpe he gradually hardened into that absolute concentration which causes one of his biographers to say that "his capacity for meditation, both in intensity and duration, has probably never been equalled", and earlier prompted his amanuensis to write that during his set times for working "his diligence . . . made me think he aimed at something beyond the reach of human art and industry".

The Olympian grandeur of Newton's mind might well set off in smaller minds the memory of those lines from "The Prelude" in which Wordsworth recalls how, when on vacation from Cambridge, he suddenly realized that

> bond unknown to me
> Was given, that I should be, else sinning greatly,
> A dedicated Spirit.

Carlyle, however little he came to think of Newton, thought still less of poets. Keats, for instance: "the kind of man that Keats was", he said, "gets ever more horrible to me"; his structure of soul marked him down, for Carlyle, as a "chosen vessel of Hell". Wordsworth he found "a genuine man, which is much, but also essentially a small genuine man"; and his talk—"for prolixity, thinness, endless dilution, it excels all the other speech I had heard from mortals". Time has not confirmed these judgements. Nor did it give to Carlyle what it gave to Wordsworth—the blessing of

> an old age serene and bright
> And lovely as a Lapland night,

not to speak of what Leigh Hunt saw in Wordsworth as an old man—"a cheerful air of animal as well as spiritual confidence, and a gallant bearing, curiously reminding me of the Duke of Wellington". Our present concern is however with Wordsworth at the beginning of his life, and with Wordsworth House at Cockermouth, where he was born on 7th April, 1770. His sister Dorothy was born there on Christmas Day of the following year.

Cockermouth is not a grand town. Its single wide street suggests the mining and industrial towns to the west rather than the resorts of pleasure which lie to the east. It is in fact something of a surprise to come, in this town of cottages and mills, upon the Cumbrian Georgian splendour of Wordsworth House. This was built in 1745 for the then Sheriff of Cumberland and was let to John Wordsworth by William Earl of Lonsdale. The poet's father was then estate and law agent to Lord Lonsdale. Externally the house has the severity of the surrounding landscape, though the windows, with their moulded stone architraves, and the cast lead dated waterheads show a fastidious taste. Inside there is a real magnificence, though none of the rooms is very large. The heavy dentilled cornices, plasterwork and wide fielded panelling fall upon the eye with an effect of poetry; this nursling of the best period of English domestic building should be, in its own right, a place of pilgrimage. For the children, however, the garden, and the river which bounded it, were more exactly remembered; its terrace was their empire, and the swift flowing Derwent, afoam in its fall from the mountains, the source of their favourite games. Wordsworth's father owned a field on the opposite side of the river. This may still be reached by way of a footbridge, and its butterflies and yellow groundsel survive to please a later generation. Cockermouth Castle, now islanded among the "inconsiderable manufactories" by which (according to Murray) the town is supported, is also little changed; and one may reproduce for oneself the sensations of mystery and disciplinary fear by which Wordsworth's "young thoughts became acquainted with the grave". This house at Cockermouth preserves, I think, to a very unusual degree the ambience of those who grew up in and near it. One may regret that Gray, the most difficile of travellers, did not have time to look round the town when he visited it in September, 1767, the year following that of the Wordsworths' arrival; he had made his way "over stupendous hills" to the town, but his companion grew sick with asthma, and they had instantly to go "peppering back thro Keswick to Penrith". It is safe to say that few travellers in our own time will wish to pepper back in any hurry from this enchanting house.

Coleridge, even more than Wordsworth, was out of favour at Cheyne Row.

Everything was against him; even his attitude to Germany—Klopstock he thought "a very *German* Milton indeed" and of the Germans in general he said, "Love is the vital air of my genius, and I have not seen one human being in Germany whom I can conceive it possible for me to love, no, not one." For this reason a whole flight of Scottish darts was released against him; at best he was "a helpless Psyche overspun with Church of England cobwebs —a weak, diffuse, weltering, ineffectual man! Never was so much apparatus got ready for thinking, and so little thought." Between them, however, the two despised poets, Wordsworth and Coleridge, contrived during the years 1797 and 1798 to make of a little cottage at Nether Stowey, in Somerset, a staging-point not only in the road from Bridgwater to Watchet, but in the history of English poetry.

Coleridge first went to Stowey in July, 1794. His friend Thomas Poole, a prosperous and democratic tanner, invited him there to discuss a project for migration to America. Twelve men and twelve women, if carefully chosen, might make of America a new Arcadia, it was thought, where two or three hours' work a day would leave them free at other times to study, debate and bring up model children. Poole descried in Coleridge "the want of those inferior abilities which are necessary to the rational discharge of the common duties of life"; but he took to him none the less, and in May, 1796 he and other friends of Coleridge combined to offer the poet a sum of forty pounds annually for seven years. The "dear gutter of Stowey" became for him the symbol of an ideal peasant-life; his children, as they accumulated at regular intervals, would grow up in perfect simplicity, "their food, dress and habits completely rustic". Politics he would abjure; his "squeaking baby-trumpet of sedition" would be put aside; "I am not fit", he said, "for public life; yet the light shall stream to a far distance from my cottage window". Poole wondered if so great a monologist would not suffer from solitary confinement, remote from printers, libraries and general society. Coleridge replied that he would have six companions: "my Sara, my babe, my own shaping and disquisitive mind, my books, my beloved friend Thomas Poole, and lastly Nature looking at me with a thousand looks of beauty, and speaking to me in a thousand melodies of love". This comprehensive party settled at Nether Stowey on December the 31st, 1796.

There was great happiness there. A visitor who came to them in August, 1797 said, "I have seen domestic life in all its beauty and simplicity, affection founded on a much stronger basis than wealth—on esteem." Coleridge himself was very pleased; in a poem to his brother he wrote:

> beside one Friend,
> Beneath the impervious covert of one oak,
> I've raised a lowly shed, and know the names
> Of Husband and of Father.

When Coleridge was first married, he had not been very clever about the house; he had had, for instance, to send for a great variety of objects—"one tin dustpan; one carpet brush; one flower dredge; a pair of slippers; a cheese toaster; a bible; two large tin spoons; a keg of porter; coffee; raisins; currants;

100   Mr. and Mrs. Carlyle at Home in Cheyne Row. From the painting by Robert Tait (1857-9) in the collection of the Marquess of Northampton

101　Willy Lott's Cottage, Flatford Mill, Suffolk

102　Newton's Birthplace: Woolsthorpe Manor House, Lincolnshire

catsup; nutmegs; . . ." At Stowey things were better ordered. The house itself was not perfect; a chimney smoked, and might have to be Rumfordized (according to the method of Count Rumford, a town-planning essayist and temporary pundit); there were mice. But Coleridge was very content; he also in general found himself liked; he amused the rustics with puns and conundrums, danced with them, and even listened to what they said. His child Hartley seemed to him "a very seraph in clouts". And in the summer of 1797 there began that constant association with William and Dorothy Words worth which caused him once to say that they were in truth "three persons and one soul".

One may too easily take one's idea of Coleridge's talk from the drawing of Max Beerbohm which shows the poet haranguing a tumulus or human mound of listeners overtaken by sleep. A true idea (or one gained at this Stowey period), must surely have had in it something of the bodily exuberance which allowed Coleridge to walk forty miles and think nothing of it, or to come run ning over Helvellyn to Rydal; then something of the voice, rising "like a steam of rich, distilled perfumes", the sounds "echoing from the bottom of the human heart"; and then the electric vivacity of a mind, quick and slight as a whippet, yet with no lack of mass and gravity. The three friends completed and sus tained each other to perfection; Coleridge found Wordsworth "a very great man, the only man to whom at all times and in all modes of excellence I feel myself inferior", and his sister "a woman indeed!

> " In every motion her most innocent soul
> Outbeams so brightly, that who saw would say,
> Guilt was a thing impossible to her.

"Her information various—her eye watchful in minutest observation of nature— and her taste a perfect electrometer—it bends, protrudes, and draws in, at subtlest beauties and most recondite faults." For his part Wordsworth as an old man was to remember Coleridge at this time, and how he was "most wonderful in the power he possessed of throwing out in profusion grand central truths from which might be evolved the most comprehensive systems". The country side never failed them; "there is everything here", Dorothy Wordsworth once wrote, "sea, woods wild as fancy ever painted, brooks clear and pebbly as in Cumberland, villages so romantic; and William and I, in a wander by our selves found out a sequestered waterfall in a dell formed by steep hills covered with full-grown timber-trees. The woods are as fine as those at Lowther, and the country more romantic; it has the character of the less grand parts of the neighbourhood of the Lakes." For Coleridge the country between Holford and the Bristol Channel became nothing less than an elaborate allegory of human experience; he conceived in fact a long philosophical poem upon a stream, "traced from its source in the hills among the yellow-red moss and conical glass-shaped tufts of bent, to the first break or fall, where its drops become audible, and it begins to form a channel"—and so to the sea. This poem was not written; but others (*Kubla Khan* and *The Ancient Mariner*) were written in its place, and serve to fix this little cottage in the hearts of those who care for poetry.

16

Geographically it is not a great way from Stowey to Clouds Hill, near Bovingdon in Dorsetshire, where T. E. Lawrence lived intermittently from 1923 till his death in 1935. It would be difficult however to conceive a deeper or wider gulf than that which separates the two in their human associations. Lawrence is, I think, as purely contemporary a figure as one can imagine; he could not be pictured in any other period, and it is likely that future historians will seize on him for this very particularity.   Clouds Hill will be useful to them; for Lawrence imposed upon it his own stamp.   It was bought in October, 1923, on an overdraft; the country was familiar to him as an exercise-ground for tanks, but he came later to take pride in its oaks, laurels, rhododendrons, birches and single ilex. The cottage still contains the divan, armchair and bookrest which he designed for himself; "I have had great satisfaction", he wrote, "in building everything that goes into the place—fenders, chairs, table, couches. It has two rooms, and two of everything . . . the whole place is designed for just the single inhabitant! It has neither rugs nor paint nor plaster nor wallpaper. Panelling, bookshelves, bare wood and undyed leather. No ornaments and no pictures. A queer place, but great fun." Above the door, an allusion to Hippoclides implied that this was to be a retreat free from care. Lawrence enjoyed such embellishments as the ram, by which water was pumped fifty feet uphill through a pipe a hundred yards long—and not less because the water, when first persuaded through, tasted of "galvanized iron and red lead". Mr. E. M. Forster has described the life led at Clouds Hill— the irregular meals, eaten standing, and from tins; the gramophone concerts; the days in which it was possible to discern that, for all his devotion to the Arabs, he "belonged body and soul to our islands". He has also warned us against any too rapid judgment of Lawrence, who could so easily become "a tattoo master's asset, the boy scout's hero and the girl guide's dream".

Mr. Bernard Shaw, who is not built by nature for sitting on fences, at one time told Lawrence that his enlistment in the ranks was "shocking tomfoolery". "Nelson, cracked after his whack on the head at the battle of the Nile, coming home and insisting on being placed at the tiller of a canal barge, and on being treated as nobody in particular, would have embarrassed the Navy far less." Lawrence took this very amiably; and when Mr. Shaw embodied him in *Too True to be Good* he thought the play "magnificent; Tempestlike, almost, as a valediction". Lawrence, also forthright in his judgements, said of Mrs. Shaw that "she and G. B. S. mix like bacon and eggs into a quintessential dream. I would rather visit them than read any book or hear any music on earth." Mr. Shaw has not yet written his *Tempest*, and one may hope that not for a long time will his house at Ayot St. Lawrence be other than potentially a museum.

Mr. Shaw's unpublished work includes a number of rhymes to accompany picture postcards of Ayot St. Lawrence. One of these, bearing on the obverse a picture of the town's graveyard, runs as follows:

> Tread softly, Nell. Here Ayot's deaders
> Into eternity take headers.

These rhymes were written in 1916, when Ellen Terry and Bernard Shaw had been in correspondence for twenty-four years. Their letters, so startling in their intensity to those who have never been within "the magnetic field of the theatrical profession", are perhaps the best memorial of this great actress. Ellen Terry never lost the aerial beauty of face and utterance of which so many observers have spoken; nor did she lose the child's eye which caused her to pin down, after many years, only one incident from her honeymoon with Watts—that, on their wedding journey, he had said to her "Don't cry; it makes your nose swell." So perishable are even the greatest moments of the stage that a particular pathos attaches to all visible leavings of its past; and at Smallhythe Place, near Tenterden, is preserved such a mass of tokens, objects and curiosities as makes, for all who enjoy the theatre, an unforgettable visit.

Constable enjoyed the theatre, but he seldom went there. He also enjoyed the diorama, an amusement so much favoured by foreign visitors to London that Constable felt himself to be "in a cage of magpies". Nevertheless he thought it "without the pale of the art, because its object is deception. The art", he went on, "pleases by reminding, not by deceiving." In his own art he reminds us of the drama of landscape—a spectacle which he found more engrossing than any play. Not that he liked spectacular country. A two-months' tour in Westmorland and Cumberland served only to disenchant him of such solitudinous Alpine scenes. He turned instead to his home-ground, East Anglia; of this he said, "I even love every stile and stump, and every lane in the village, so deep-rooted are early impressions". In summer he lived almost wholly in the fields, seeing only the harvesters; even at night he would continue to sketch indoors, or to study the specimens of earth and stone which, as his brother records, he was always careful to take home. Mills and mill-houses attracted him above all; he even developed the windmiller's eye, and finely describes how from a great mass of clouds one may pick out those isolated patches of vapour which "are called by windmillers and sailors, *messengers*, and always portend bad weather". When travelling he would find his way, as if by instinct, to "the *mill*, surrounded by weirs, back-waters, nets and willows; with a smell of weeds, flowing water and flour in my nostrils". His last picture, and the one on which he worked on the last day of his life, was of a mill; and of all such he loved best Dedham and Flatford mills, and the mill of Willy Lott's house. Sir Kenneth Clark, in writing of *The Hay-Wain*, has pointed out that for Constable Willy Lott's house was a symbol of rustic peace. (Constable's biographer, C. R. Leslie, remarks that Willy Lott was born in the house, and for more than eighty years never spent four whole days away from it.) This small house, which in itself is nothing out of the way, was the subject of a series of sketches and paintings as remarkable as any in the history of landscape. Curiously enough Constable, writing in 1827 of a painting by Ruysdael, exactly voices our own impressions of *The Hay-Wain*. "I have seen an affecting picture this morning . . . it haunts my mind, and clings to my heart . . . it is a water-mill; a man and boy are cutting rushes in the running stream (the tail-water); the whole so true, clear, fresh and brisk as champagne; a shower has not long passed." For Constable, each hour of the day had its own character, and he was never weather-bound; but in *The Hay-Wain* it is the solemnity of a summer noon which binds and supports its giant design. Constable knew well what he was about; and he recognized in Gilbert White, for instance, a fellow-traveller. One might say of him, as he says of White, that "the single page of his life leaves a more lasting impression on my mind than all that has been written of Charles V or any other removed hero". Painting was for him "but another word for feeling"; and he was in line with a great tradition of English poetry. "The sound of water escaping from mill-dams, etc., willows, old rotten planks, slimy posts, and brickwork, I love such things. Shakespeare could make everything poetical; he tells us of poor Tom's haunts among 'sheep cotes and mills'. As long as I do paint, I shall never cease to paint such things." No tour of secular shrines could be complete without some mention of Willy Lott's house; obsolete and poky as it may be, no building in England is more surely a national trust.

103 Bernard Shaw's House at Ayot St. Lawrence, Hertfordshire

104 Ellen Terry's Home: the Priest's House, Smallhythe, Kent

105 Seals on the Farne Islands, Northumberland

106 Guillemots on the Farne Islands

107 Cormorants Nesting on the Farne Islands

108 Puffins on the Farne Islands

109 The Pinnacles, Farne Islands, Northumberland

X

NATURE RESERVES

By Sir William Beach Thomas

SANCTUARY is a pleasant word, and it is pleasant to know of places where animals (from badgers to butterflies) and indeed precious flowers are safe in unspoilt scenes, and perhaps on the way to multiply. More than this, the sanctuary is a home where the presence of this life can be securely studied and enjoyed.

Sanctuaries of one sort or another are scattered widely over England though the eastern side is better equipped than the west or north. Some of them are owned by one person, such as Fallodon, some by a group of people, such as Hickling Broad, some by local trusts, such as the Cley Marshes, some by the National Trust which may or may not share the responsibility with others. Now we are used to regard a sanctuary as a rather small place with a strict definition; and often the protected animals know the boundaries very precisely. Ducks at Fallodon may be quite tame within the pale and quite wild as soon as they cross beyond the boundary. The same perception is recorded of lions in the Kruger Park in South Africa. Now the increased interest of the National Trust in nature reserves gives hope of a wider conception of the word. Every country place permanently preserved by the National Trust is in some sort a sanctuary, as almost every private garden is a sanctuary, a place where birds and plants and butterflies are safe from most mortal dangers. But before discussing this newer development it may be well to look at a few sanctuaries to which the preciser definition applies; and some of the possessions of the Trust are among the best models in the world of what such a well-defined sanctuary should be. Perhaps the most characteristic of all is held in beneficent co-operation with the Norfolk Naturalists' Trust, a real pioneer in the making and supporting of nature preserves. Scolt Head, so called, has all the advantages. It is, in Tennyson's phrase, an almost-island saved by its narrow and precarious connection with the mainland from dangerous trespass, whether by man or vermin. That invaluable custodian, the Watcher, has a comparatively easy task, though he is kept busy enough. The pre-eminence of Scolt Head is due to a number of its attributes. It has been more exhaustively surveyed than any well-defined area in Britain with one exception. Its tides and soil and weather as well as the biology of its plants and animal life have been scientifically studied. It is on a line of drift or migration. It is my experience that you can watch there the process of migration, for example, of the wheatear, as in few other places. It has great attraction for some of the northern birds, such as the snow-bunting as well as such early arrivals from the south as the wheatear; and that ardent bird-watcher, Miss Turner, who lived for a long space in the hut-house by the dunes, saw there one of the multitudinous migrations of white butterflies. The great success of the sanctuary outside its native quality, is due largely to the fruitful association of the National Trust with the Norfolk Naturalists' Trust.

Its one rival in completeness of survey is Wicken Fen, every inch of which has been closely investigated, largely by young men of science from Cambridge University. It is held to be one of the very few spots within England that has not been "humanized" in the past, though the great dykes at its edge, sometimes golden with waterlilies and blue with dragonfly have acted as drains. More than this: every sanctuary needs management, such as the cutting of excessive sedge or bush and perhaps the making of drives. The moth-ers, who find Wicken Fen quite unique, set up their posts on a smooth green road through the sedges. In parts of Norfolk, where once the great copper butterfly flour-ished, some host-plants too—the water-dock for example—have been reintro-duced. But when all is said, Wicken remains a fen almost as in pre-historic times, certainly such a fen as Hereward the Wake loved and the monks of Crowland recorded. Some of the adjacent land, notably Adventurers' Fen, was reclaimed and cultivated, to the alarm of the Trust, during the war. The place retains, and may be expected to retain, its ancient form and hospitality, and remains a place of pilgrimage both for botanists and entomologists. The birds too increase.

The whole property is a preserved area under the Cambridge County Council (which prohibits egg collecting) and the Trust specially prohibits the uprooting of plants. It is of course not enough to prohibit offences of this sort. A fen especially is likely, if left to itself, to become "a tangled mass of tall coarse sedge (Cladium), strangling all growth but its own, and shaded by alien trees, which intrude and dry up the soil, until we have an almost impenetrable thicket unsuited to animal and plant life". This was almost the fate of one corner of Wicken Fen before the National Trust took it in hand. Excessive growth is thinned, and waterways kept comparatively clear, and then the native flora and fauna remain as of old. However one small bit is left virgin, un-touched, as a sort of negative proof of the need of active, not negative con-servation elsewhere.

The story of the acquirement of Wicken Sedge Fen (which is about a square mile in area) is worth recording as an example of the difficulty of preservation. On a rumour that the Sedge Fen was to be drained, a number of people particularly interested in its plants and insects bought up small bits. A little later and soon after its formation in 1895 the Trust became interested in the area and bought a small part. Among those who purchased parts of Burwell Fen and the Sedge Fen were the Hon. N. C. Rothschild, who gave all four bits of land he had bought to the Trust, and Mr. C. H. Verrall, who bequeathed no less than 239 acres of Wicken Sedge to the Trust. These salient examples of generosity of naturalists, and indeed local historians, proved contagious. The possessions of the Trust by gift and purchase have increased, but the reclamation of Adventurers' Fen during the war, and more especially the demands of agriculture are not unlikely to arrest further enlargement. The preserved areas under control of the Trust now include not only "the undisturbed ground in Wicken Sedge Fen" but valuable bits of Burwell and St. Edmund's Fens. The treatment of the neighbourhood may affect any sanctuary, and neighbouring essays in draining threaten some dangers to Wicken. It would be a disaster, for example, if greater dryness were to destroy the not very common milk parsley which is the host-plant of the swallow-tail butterfly, which still flourishes in Wicken Fen, but the botanists say that this weed as well as the marsh fern, the marsh pea and the yellow loosestrife thrive where the sedge is kept in check, and "show a decided tendency to increase now that the Trust is looking after their interest".

Most nature reserves protect plants as well as living creatures. Perhaps no place is more famous as a reserve for particular species of birds than Blakeney Spit; but there and at Scolt Head and in the other areas of marsh and shingle, more exclusively under the control of the Norfolk naturalists, the list of rarer plants also is of peculiar interest; but at Blakeney and at Scolt Head the birds matter most, as the plants and insects at Wicken. It is a quaint feature of parts of the Norfolk and Suffolk coasts that their sand and shingle banks arrest the direct progress of the rivers which thereupon are forced to flow, often for a mile or two parallel with the shore and close to it before they find their way into the sea. The spits so formed especially at Blakeney, provide their optimum, their best possible conditions, for the nesting of the terns or sea-swallows. Just above high water along a favourite stretch of beach the nests of terns, more especially sandwich terns are packed so closely together that you have difficulty in dodging them with your feet, and when the young are hatched, the disturbed and angry parents fly close over your head till they shut out the sun like the threatened arrows at Thermopylae. The cries are confused and almost deafening, but some watchers have cultivated so acute a sense of hearing and are so full of experience that they can detect the difference of cry coming from the sandwich tern, which especially delights in the place, and other terns which from time to time include a pair or so of the rare and lovely roseate tern. Other sea birds find harbourage there, not least the oyster-catcher, but Blakeney is first and foremost a tern sanctuary, and these birds need very particular conditions: they are fastidious. Their nesting home pleases them better even than the Chesil Bank at Abbotsbury where they may enjoy the luxury of a brackish bath. In no other part of England does tide so alter the scenery. As it rises it runs up the brooks and over the low land at an altogether surprising speed, till the whole surface changes before your eyes through marsh to lake and the sea-swallows fly up to the high-tide mark the better part of a mile inland. The keepers of the reserves hereabouts have trouble from time to time with collectors both of eggs and the bodies of the birds themselves; but next to none from the collectors of plants. The case is exactly reversed in parts of more northern England. A good example may be found in the records of the delightful but less important sanctuary of Hawksmoor in Staffordshire, which was first secured by the zeal and energy of Mr. Masefield, a relation of the Poet Laureate. It lies alongside a very favourite picnic place of urban holiday-makers; and it became a question how far the reserve should be left open to the public. Part of it is a well treed and well-bushed dell, beautiful in itself but not naturally congenial to the tripper. Some hopeful persons had faith enough that the public would respect the quality of sanctuary and not unduly disturb birds and beasts, if a special regulation was made for the comparatively few weeks of the nesting season. The faith may one day be justified, but it has failed in one regard. Ferns have a curious fascination for our north country people and the sanctuary has lost one of its more attractive species. In other respects it is sanctuary indeed in spite of its popularity with a large number of visitors. The idea of it was not only to preserve native plants but to provide a garden for them, and in this reference it has been most successful except for the little harts-tongue. But makers of such reserves always also accumulate an "unearned increment". This includes at Hawksmoor families of that shy animal the badger and the red squirrel, a species that had been diminishing at any rate in Southern and Eastern England. The many birds that delight in the place have met two rather surprising enemies: bees and wasps drive them from a number of the nesting boxes provided for their uses. A number of these nesting boxes were made for the Trust by schoolboys (who are often keen and good carpenters); and it is hoped to extend this practice. Such work is more than doubly blessed. It encourages a desirable craft, teaches the young idea the value of preservation and helps to provide useful paraphernalia for sanctuary keepers. As to human disturbance, the suggestion to enforce quiet for thirteen weeks during the breeding season may prove a complete solution of the alleged impossibility of combining accessibility with protection. The war has in some measure interfered with the sanctity of the sanctuary as with most other things. The order has gone forth that trees must be felled and Staffordshire, with some other inland places, has suffered severely. The process has entailed disturbance; and the natural balance has been in some measure upset. However, few birds, butterflies, or for that matter mammals depend much on the larger trees. Even tree-nesting birds are willing enough to fall back on lesser growths. A necessity of many sanctuaries is the watcher; and he deserves his name more than the so-called keeper, who may be a destroyer, prouder of his "larder" than of the rarer birds.

The war has interfered with the smooth progress of protection, though it has not interfered with the extension of the National Trust, and it was found necessary to close down, from 1939 to 1943, the Natural History Advisory Committee and most of its work. But the emphasis on protection does not diminish. The Trust of course remains in the first place a preserver "in perpetuity" of places of historic and national interest, not least in respect of architecture, and what may be called the architecture of the landscape fills a larger place in its activities. Men used to seek sanctuary within a sacred building; but someone wrote with pardonable metaphor of

> Column and arch and architrave
> And all the tricks that builders learned of trees.

The gardens and paddocks and farms, the woods and spinneys and groves which belong to the buildings given over to the Trust are beginning to be treated as the sacred homes of mammals, insects and flowers, not only for the sake of their preservation but for their study, for the encouragement of natural

110   Sandwich Terns on the Farne Islands

111   Terns and Oyster Catchers nesting at Blakeney Point, Norfolk

112 Wicken Sedge Fen, Cambridgeshire

113 Birches on Hawksmoor, Staffordshire

history and its young historians. It may be argued that the more the knowledge of natural history is spread abroad the more our people will desire to preserve mammal, bird and flower, as well as landscape beauty. It has been noticed in the neighbourhood of Hickling Broad (a great but private sanctuary) that the people who live round about become, so to say, sanctuary-minded. The keepers do not shoot harriers and farmers regard owls with favour; but, alas, it is not a general experience. Where game are highly preserved, though many of the inhabitants grow proud of the great rare birds that may be seen about their homes, hawks, harriers, owls and even such harmless birds as the bitterns are still ruthlessly shot. What is of surpassing importance is that children should be brought up to be sanctuary-minded.

Children are naturally fond of birds; but too often, like game preservers, in the vein of Tom Tulliver, who was very fond of birds, "that is of throwing stones at them", or of robbing their nests. All the possessions of the National Trust, it may be claimed, are in some sort educational, with apologies for that severe word. They extend the knowledge of history, at the same time that they preserve its documentary evidence, so to speak. This may be said of a particular building, but it is at least as true (or is going to be at least as true) in respect of the rural scene, not only in acres definitely established as natural history sanctuaries, but wherever mammal, bird, butterfly or plant may flourish. Indeed the lead in this more or less new conception of the scope of the National Trust is likely to be taken by a spot that was given to the Trust in the first instance for its close association with English art and artists. Flatford Mill is famous of course as the home of the young Constable, perhaps the greatest of all our painters of the rural scene. Incidentally it may be recorded that when he was apprenticed to the Suffolk miller he used to be sent out to discover just where the wind was and what it was likely to be. This part of his duty encouraged him to be an observer of clouds—as well as rainbows—and among the smaller and less well-known sketches of his younger days are many studies of cloud over Flatford Mill some of which have recently been picked up by American buyers.

Now during the war and in despite of the war, a Cambridge naturalist came to the conclusion that there was a great need for improving, for enlarging the facilities for so-called field studies. The phrase is too narrow on the face of it, not least if it is quoted in connection with Flatford Mill. The response to his suggestions on ways and means of helping students and observers of natural history was so wide and eager that it led to the formation of a body now named the "Council for the Promotion of Field Studies". The central idea of the council was to open, as soon as possible after the war, a number of Field Centres in different parts of the country, where students could be cheaply housed and given opportunity and help in the pursuit of their hobby, if the word may be used of semi-scientific study. How could such centres be acquired? It was natural for the Council to get into touch with the National Trust and they found sympathetic hearing. Indeed their approach coincided with an extension of the scope of the Trust itself. The idea was that each centre should be "staffed and suitably equipped to provide adequate board, lodging and working facilities for numbers ranging up to 40 or 50 students, each centre to be under the direction of a Warden, who will be a trained field observer and an experienced naturalist, with wide cultural sympathies".

There is in existence no single association except the Natural Trust, in a position to offer suitable centres in widely separated districts; and the National Trust proved whole-heartedly sympathetic towards the idea. So a scheme came into being, by which the Council should lease National Trust properties for their particular purpose. It is thought that the arrangement would be every way beneficial: the Warden and his flock would attend to the work of pre-serving the leased properties as national monuments and at least ensure the Trust (which is not a rich organization) against loss of money. It is probable that the Board of Education and perhaps the universities will give grants for maintenance and so enable the naturalists to pay adequate sums for their privileges. The Trust was more than sympathetic. It made a definite offer to the Council of the lease of Flatford Mill in East Suffolk. The abundant and quiet streams of this district make it only less popular with birds than the Broads of Norfolk, which are the greatest paradise of birds within the island. It is the habitat of very many plants not generally common and there is of course abundant life in the water. So Flatford Mill is likely to become popular not only for its history in art. It should become a pioneer centre where experi-ence may be gained for a new sort of study of natural history. Already a "unique collection of natural history material" has been presented for the use of coming students at the Flatford Mill Field Centre.

Among the main purposes of the Trust as laid down are the preservation of natural beauty and of wild life; and this work of preserving wild life was never narrowed to the compass of a sanctuary in the strict sense. Many of the best sanctuaries are comparatively small, such as the admirable little reserve associated with the name of Ruskin by Abingdon or—though this is not on Trust property—the delightfully compact spinney at Whipsnade where English birds may be seen over the head of Amherst pheasants from the China Seas or the brush turkey from Australia. Many places belonging to the Trust, and not regarded principally as nature reserves, make the naturalist's mouth water. A certain "clump" by Maidenhead, for example, is remembered vividly by more than one ornithologist as the first place where they found a nest of the hawfinch. The West of England—in general as in the sphere of the Trust's activities—is much less well sprinkled with nature reserves than the East; but some of the Trust's possessions regarded in essence as providing space for recreation and refreshment of body and mind for the general public, are also a proper object of pilgrimage for naturalists. For example one of the strangest incidents in wild life ever witnessed by the present writer was at Baggy Point in North Devon where a greater black-backed gull flew out from the cliff to deliver a savage attack on two herons flying over the sea a few hundred yards away. More than this; he and others have made an almost annual journey to the Point to watch from amid the pink thrift lining the cliff the peaceable nesting of the herring gulls below. After the same fashion the beautiful and popular walk on the other wing of the bay at Morte Point is remembered as a favourite haunt of the buzzards and as a taking-off ground for great flocks of migrating swallows. Farther north again on the west coast, those parts of Pembrokeshire and its islands with which the Trust has any concern are a paradise for birds. The cliffs are especially popular with the peregrine; and close to the nest of this most beautiful falcon some of us have found the nest of that rare bird, the red-legged chough and on the rocky shore the eggs of the oyster-catcher reposing (rather against the common habit of the species) on a thick, well-made nest of lichen. It is, I think, a fact of general application that wherever the Trust comes into possession of any rural—or for that matter semi-rural—land there the birds and flowers get a better chance of survival. The success of many sanctuaries, in the strict sense of the term, has depended a good deal on the "watcher", the man appointed to live by the spot with the special purpose of preventing collectors (who are of many sorts) or casual and local sportsmen, so-called, disturbing the sanctity of the ground; and it is to be hoped that the Trust and its agents in the wider possessions will find among local naturalists men (or women) who can play the part of the official watcher.

In the pursuit of its ideals—which are the ideals of all naturalists—it is inevitable that the Trust should have dealings with other bodies and persons who have narrower objects and as a rule the results have been welcome to naturalists. One example occurred at that most historic of the Trust's sanctu-aries at Wicken Fen on the occasion of schemes for reclaiming land up to the edge of the sanctuary and thus in some measure interfering with its sanctity. An admirable example of the results of friendly discussion in the arrangement with the Forestry Commission (which has ideals which conflict very sharply with those of naturalists, especially local naturalists) in the Lakes. Has not Eskdale and the Duddon Valley been declared a National Forest Park ?

In regard to the properties of the Trust that are specifically labelled as sanctu-aries some of course have been acquired rather by the accident of circumstance than because of any peculiar qualities, such, for example, as Selsdon Wood in Surrey, though the place both by its position and clothing, is rich in bird-life, especially perhaps migrant warblers. What a district it is, in spite of being a populous district, for the study of birds' song! Much the same may be said of the Chase, Woolton Hill, Newbury. But Berkshire, like Surrey, is a favourite with particular birds. For example, the neighbourhood of Newbury is—in the experience of some naturalists—peculiarly attractive to that now, alas! rare bird, the wryneck.

These smaller and less well-known sanctuaries are dotted about the country more or less at haphazard. They will certainly multiply at the bequest of individual owners who wish a certain rare flower or bird in which they specially delight to enjoy security in perpetuity. On the other hand most if not all the bigger sanctuaries are widely recognized as possessing particular or indeed peculiar claims to protection. Blakeney Point and Scolt Head, as I have said have scarcely any parallel in the island in regard to their form and structure, which in turn draws to its attraction certain birds and encourages certain plants. The "blessed word" ecology is the word of the moment in natural history discussions. Every naturalist is forced to be or pretend to be, an ecologist, a student of the influence of surroundings on animal and plant. The Farne Islands, where a kittiwake colony flourishes, are not less individual than Blakeney with its terns, and Scolt Head with its snow-bunting and the rest. Some years ago a young research worker decided that the Farne Islands were the only place where he could find the conditions he sought and he made there a number of curious observations especially on the habits of gulls of several species, as well as on domestic poultry! They have advantages possessed not even by Skokholm, made rightly famous by Mr. Lockley. These islands are perhaps in certain important respects one of the most valuable of all reserves. One great scientific naturalist considers that they are, or will be, the most important in the whole of Western Europe without exception. Very much in the same way as it is necessary to destroy excessive sedge and bushes in Wicken Fen, it is necessary in the Farnes to reduce the numbers of the more savage gulls: the greater and lesser blackbacks and indeed the herring gulls which take terrible toll of the eggs and young of Arctic, Sandwich and roseate terns, eider duck, puffins, fulmars and many others. To the birds which find a natural home in the Farnes must be added a number of plants and, not least, the Atlantic seal.

The nearest parallel on the west coast is perhaps the Calf of Man. This compact little island of just over 615 acres is ringed like the Farne Islands with rocks. It is rather less popular than the Farnes with some species perhaps because its contrast with its bigger neighbour is less abrupt. The south end of the Isle of Man has some of the finest cliffs—and views—within Britain. The Farnes on the other hand attract birds that are apt to shun the sandy flats of Northumberland. (On the Farnes the gulls are given their optimum of conditions including the privacy proper to a sanctuary.)

The number of naturalists within Britain seems to grow yearly. Some of them have their private sanctuaries, which they would wish to be continuously preserved after their time. So it is more than probable that more and more small reserves will come under the control of the Trust just as stretches or nests of beautiful landscape consistently multiply. Naturalists will unite in rejoicing not only in the multiplication but in the nature of the ownership. After all the Council of the Trust is very definitely represented by naturalists. Members are nominated by the Society for the Preservation of Nature Reserves, by the Royal Entomological Society, the Linnaean Society, the Royal Botanic Society and the Selborne Society. As to Selborne, the lovely and famous hill may be considered as one of the "almost-sanctuaries" possessed by the National Trust. People in general are a little apt to associate the word sanctuary with the protection of birds, but the very titles of the societies that nominate members to the Council indicate how various are the sorts of natural history that need reserves and in which the Trust is semi-officially interested. We need mammal sanctuaries, insect sanctuaries and plant sanctuaries no less than bird sanctuaries and it is possible for those who have control of nature reserves to cultivate as well as to protect. One good example is the planting of a once almost extinct species of dock at Wicken Fen and other eastern districts in order that it may serve for host to the Great Copper Butterfly. It is an open question whether the naturalization of, say, vanished butterflies should be attempted in order to make good as far as possible regrettable losses. But the widsom of such restitution may safely be left to the Trust. All manner of fine points crop up in the management of sanctuaries, the extent of the cutting, for example of sedges and bushes after the manner practised most successfully at Wicken Fen and Hickling Broad and uprooting of such aliens as the quick, which is intrusive everywhere. It may perhaps be thought that such technical points are too small to be given proper attention by an organization possessing such spacious and varied properties and interested at least as much in scenery and architecture as in natural history. Nevertheless the Trust is more definitely naturalist than most people think. The full title after all is "The National Trust for Places of Historic Interest or Natural Beauty". Is there room under this for encouragement of the Great Copper Butterfly or the Bearded Tit? The answer is in the affirmative. The overmastering success of Scolt Head as a reserve, especially for birds and plants and as a centre of research is due to the close collaboration with local naturalists as with Cambridge botanists, entomologists and geologists at Wicken and young men of science, especially from the universities. So great a central body as the National Trust is in a position not only to make surveys but to enter into common trust with other bodies more directly concerned with the technical details of natural history. The supreme debt that naturalists owe and will come to owe to the National Trust in large measure is in the first place of course that the reserves are saved in perpetuity; but there are other forms of debt. After all the developing idea within the Trust is to extend the sanctuary spirit in the preservation of animals and plants as in the wider sphere of scenic beauty and historic value. The areas in which students can have liberty for field observation grow with the accumulating possessions of the Trust as the creatures and plants within them grow more secure. This is a general truth apart from such definite adventures as that meditated at Flatford Mill, where old and historic houses may serve as hostels for natural historians, whether students in a strict interest or pursuers of the best of hobbies. As the possessions of the Trust increase, increases the perception of how much may be done to further the spirit that was the first cause of the Trust's creation. That the educational value of the reserve is hardly less important than its research value is one of the tenets of the Trust; and we may expect to see cumulative results from this faith. A visit to a sanctuary may be in the nature of a liberal education, for child or grownup.

THE WORK OF THE NATIONAL TRUST

By D. M. MATHESON
Secretary of the National Trust

IT is only within comparatively recent times that either the need or the duty to preserve what was best of England's legacy of wilder beauty and of historic buildings revealed itself as in any degree urgent. The industrial revolution turned England more and more into the workshop of the world, and improving means of transport brought more and more of the country within easy reach of the growing towns.

In the mid-nineteenth century there was a widespread belief that commercial expansion, peace, general well-being and prosperity would go forward hand in hand. As a result, emotional and philanthropic sanctions were extended to any development of property expected to increase its economic value. Common lands (no longer used by commoners), to which there had been customary access for the general public, were often capable of "improvement" by building development, and the economic argument for sweeping away any legal obstacles seemed unanswerable. Where old buildings could be replaced by something up-to-date capable of yielding a satisfactory return on the outlay, the lost value of beauty seemed of little account compared with the advancement of prosperity.

But there were other forces at work, by which the National Trust was ultimately to be brought into being. The Romantic Movement had drawn attention to the beauties of uncultivated nature. And John Ruskin, John Stuart Mill, T. H. Huxley, William Morris and others finally helped to bring into being the Commons Preservation Society (1865) and the Society for the Protection of Ancient Buildings (1877). The Commons Society served to rouse a strong public feeling against the further enclosure of commons by its vigorous defence of Hampstead Heath, of Berkhamsted, Plumstead, Tooting, Wandsworth and Wimbledon Commons and of Epping and Ashdown Forests. The S.P.A.B.—the Anti-Scrape, as it came to be called—also conducted a lively campaign against ill-conceived restoration or alteration of ancient buildings.

Cases arose in which land or an old building could be "saved" if it could be put into safe hands for the future, and three remarkable people determined to found a permanent Trust for that purpose. They were Octavia Hill, whose housing work had led her to a vivid appreciation of the value of such places as Parliament Hill Fields to the urban working classes, Sir Robert Hunter, who, as solicitor, had been closely concerned with the Commons Preservation Society since 1868, and Canon Rawnsley, then Vicar of Wray in Westmorland, who had in 1883 shown great vigour and pertinacity in opposing a threatened railway from Buttermere to Braithwaite. It was Octavia Hill who boldly proposed that the new body should be called The National Trust. The three founders made an admirable combination. Sir Robert brought legal knowledge and determination and ingenuity for overcoming difficulties; Miss Hill combined in a remarkable degree enthusiasm, philanthropy and commonsense, while Canon Rawnsley possessed unflagging energy and zeal of the kind which refuses to accept defeat.

In January, 1895, the Trust was incorporated as a public company not trading for profit, and from the first made steady progress under the Presidency, first, of the Duke of Westminster, and from 1902 of H.R.H. Princess Louise. At that time neither the Office of Works nor Local Authorities had the power or means to enable them to preserve what the Trust set out to acquire and preserve, and indeed part of the Trust's achievement has been the arousing of interest which has led the State and Local Authorities to take an ever larger part in the protection or preservation of the beauty and historic interest of our land.

The progress of the Trust can be briefly indicated by a few important events. In 1901 the first big appeal was issued—for £7,000 to buy 108 acres on the shores of Derwentwater. In 1904 this was followed by the raising of £12,800 for buying 750 acres of Gowbarrow Fell overlooking Ullswater. In 1907 a new status was acquired by the incorporation of the Trust under a special Act of Parliament. The outbreak of war in 1914 involved a temporary setback, but, immediately after the war came a new period of growth marked by the appeals for large properties at Stonehenge Downs and Ashridge. By 1934 such appeals to meet threatened development had become more difficult, and in the Buttermere Valley an experiment was made in protecting land by covenants which involved the raising of relatively smaller sums. In the same year Lord Lothian urged the Trust to formulate a scheme for preserving historic and beautiful country houses with their collections, gardens and parks. In 1937 a further Act was passed by Parliament to give the Trust additional powers for the Country Houses Scheme ultimately formulated. In 1939 yet another Act was passed extending this Scheme to settled estates.

This story of progress—continued by a growth in the area owned by the Trust from 46,500 acres at the end of 1938 to 110,000 acres at the end of 1944—is only a partial picture. The founders of the Trust obviously envisaged their object mainly as a defensive fight against despoiling by "development". Other more "offensive" aspects of the Trust's campaign have come into prominence since, though the public at large still think of the Trust as saving something from threats of destruction or development by some single and final step. In fact, preservation cannot be achieved by any single act. Even the lands and buildings protected in the past ten years by covenants will require constant watchfulness, and preservation entails much more than watchfulness.

The first new problem was that of the setting. To save some hilltop as a place of public resort, and then to see it surrounded with eyesores, makes it evident that in many cases action on a large scale is essential, action to control rather than to preserve. This control of land uses, of the location of industry and so on can only be done effectively by the State, and the State has steadily moved towards taking control through some kind of planning. To attempt to protect the beauty of the Buttermere Valley or the majesty of Stonehenge by raising great funds to buy large areas may be necessary as an emergency measure. As a permanent instrument of national policy it would be no more sensible than if the Dutch Government were to employ a party of small children to prevent inundations by plugging with their arms any holes in dykes. National planning control is the right answer. Covenants with the Trust proved a useful expedient meanwhile. Purchase by the Trust should be limited to places where there is to be a large measure of public access involving active management.

Here is indeed the second new problem. Nature is herself a despoiler. In this country the "natural aspect" is always conditioned to a considerable extent by man's operations. And preservation does not, and cannot, mean the stasis of a specimen preserved in spirit in a pathological museum; it means a highly specialized type of management and control aiming at preserving such an aspect as will be felt to be beautiful. Friar's Crag at Derwentwater is visited by so many thousands that the soil is worn away from the roots of the ageing trees which enhance its beauty. In time these trees will die. Thymey downland turf is produced by sheep-grazing. If humans and rabbits are numerous and sheep few a steady succession of changes must begin which will change the whole aspect of the downs. Ecology is a new science, and a large part of the Trust's work must now be envisaged as the practical study of a special kind of ecology. The Trust has not only to study plant successions and the inter-action of insects, birds and animals with plant life and of the visiting public with them all. It must endeavour to harmonize with all these the changing needs of land used for arable cultivation, for pasture, for woodland, etc., the welfare of tenants and the enjoyment of the public. In doing so it must envisage always the continual progress of beauty. In the case of country houses there are further special problems of retaining them as living homes and of the unobtrusive control of the visiting public. These problems have as yet hardly been tackled, so new is the Country Houses Scheme.

The Country Houses Scheme which stands financially separate from the Trust's general work has resulted in the acquisition of some land held primarily as special endowment for country houses. Other big stretches of country, including farms and villages, have been acquired apart from that scheme. The Trust has therefore a varied task. It must find a way of being a national body with a national policy, and yet remain in close touch with tenants and their needs. Endowment lands must be well managed to produce revenue. Agriculture—and especially grazing—must be con-tinued on many lands frequented by the public, if their beauty is to be retained. Other wilder lands must be artificially kept from changing to the type of primitive scrub, to which they naturally tend to revert. Old buildings must be adapted to modern needs, without losing their charm or architectural interest. All this work—hardly envisaged by the founders—involves the development of a quite specialized and new technique of estate management. To-day it represents by far the greater part of the work of the Trust, and on its success the future reputation of the Trust will largely depend.

Reference has been made to the protection of land and buildings by covenants. Nearly 40,000 acres are now protected in this way. That means the land is restricted so that certain things may not be done on it, and, if the Trust finds any owner doing anything forbidden in the covenants, it may apply for an injunction to restrain him. So far as land is concerned, further development of covenants would become less likely, if planning were effectively to cover the whole country; how far this will happen is of course still uncertain. In the case of buildings of historic interest covenants will in any event continue to be of some value, though they may prove difficult to enforce effectively. They are in effect not unlike scheduling under the Ancient Monuments Acts, but are applicable to a wider range of buildings than can in practice be covered by those Acts up to the present time. They will not ensure that the buildings are kept in repair, but only that they are not demolished, or so altered as materially to diminish their historic interest.

Behind all this lie, of course, the problems of deciding what is, from one point of view or another, worthy of preservation and, secondly, whether the Trust can afford to accept properties proposed to be acquired by it. There are also the problems of administration and finance inevitable for any undertaking with a wide field. Looking to the future we can see a tendency for the work of upkeep of buildings to become more, and for the value of the monetary endowments in terms of goods and services to decrease. Only prudent foresight can hope to maintain a financial position which will enable the Trust to continue effectively to maintain and preserve what it holds for the nation.

The contributors to this book have admirably described various aspects of the Trust's work in acquiring and managing properties, and what it has achieved in its first fifty years. Many of the properties might have been described under several sections. The Farne Islands combine historic interest with natural beauty, quite apart from their importance as a nature reserve. Wallington combines natural beauty with the interest of eighteenth-century architecture and many associations of literary interest. Polesden Lacey includes not only very valuable open spaces but a house (not itself of special interest) with a museum collection of beautiful things. As the work has grown in extent, so it has grown in complexity, but the Trust's field is now so diversified that further development in the range of difficult matters with which it has to deal is likely to be less marked.

To-day the Trust is large enough to have required reorganization with an expert staff of property managers with officers in some eight regions, not all of which can be established now. Behind the work of the staff is the generous help of a body of expert honorary advisors on all sorts of special problems connected with the properties. There must be brought to their work the eye for landscape of the artist as well as professional efficiency. However the State's control and protection of land uses may grow, there will always remain an important field for an independent body like the Trust with long special experience in the management and upkeep of an unique type of property —land and buildings held primarily for their beauty or interest, to which the public have as great a measure of access as practicable. The Trust is confident that the public will continue generously to support it so long as it shows by what it does that it can competently undertake its work. The Trust should acquire only what is of real national interest, and not already effectively cared for. The property which may be so described is limited in extent. It will be more limited still in practice, in certain localities, if national parks are set up in which a Special Commission exercises similar functions, using public funds for the purpose. There are, however, so many places of exceptional beauty or interest not owned by the Trust or any other public body that it would be no idle dream to hope that in the second fifty years the Trust will, without lowering its standards, acquire at least as many new properties as it has acquired in the first fifty.

INDEX

Those place names in heavy type are properties owned by the National Trust; those in italics are properties, not owned, but protected by means of restrictive covenants with the Trust.

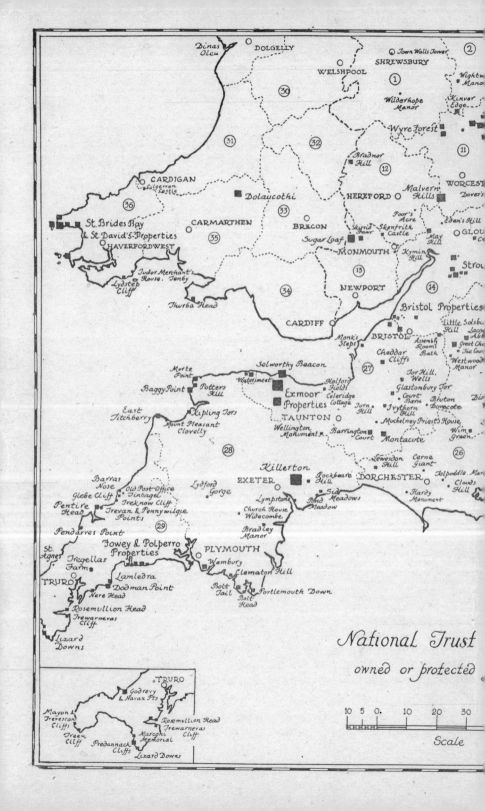

National Trust

owned or protected

National Trust Properties

owned or protected by covenant

10 5 0   10   20   30   40   50   60   miles

Scale

LE ON TYNE

Wood
oor

Saltwick Nab

HALLERTON ■
Bridestones Properties
(6)

YORK
York Properties
(8)

BEVERLEY
O

O HULL

EFIELD

Gainsborough   (9)

LINCOLN
O St. Mary's Guildhall   *Gunby Hall* ■
(10)

Edge
st House
nifold Properties
ff Wood

Tattershall Castle

BOSTON
O

Scolt Head   *Blakeney Point* ■

NOTTINGHAM
Grantham House ■
Colston Bassett ■   Woolsthorpe Manor House
Market Cross

Burnham Overy Mill   *Bale Oaks* ■   West Runton Camp ■
Bullfer Grove ■   *Blickling* ■

(15)   (14)
PETERBOROUGH
O   *Thorney Abbey House* ■

Bank House Wisbech ■

Swanton Morley ■

(13)

NORWICH
O